ASP.NET MVC 5 with Bootstrap and Knockout.js

Building Dynamic, Responsive Web Applications

Jamie Munro

Beijing · Cambridge · Farnham · Köln · Sebastopol · Tokyo

ASP.NET MVC 5 with Bootstrap and Knockout.js

by Jamie Munro

Copyright © 2015 Jamie Munro. All rights reserved.

Printed in the United States of America.

Published by O'Reilly Media, Inc., 1005 Gravenstein Highway North, Sebastopol, CA 95472.

O'Reilly books may be purchased for educational, business, or sales promotional use. Online editions are also available for most titles (*http://safaribooksonline.com*). For more information, contact our corporate/institutional sales department: 800-998-9938 or corporate@oreilly.com.

Editor: Meg Foley	**Indexer:** Wendy Catalano
Production Editor: Nicole Shelby	**Interior Designer:** David Futato
Copyeditor: Kim Cofer	**Cover Designer:** Ellie Volckhausen
Proofreader: Marta Justak	**Illustrator:** Rebecca Demarest

May 2015:   First Edition

Revision History for the First Edition

2015-05-08:   First Release

See *http://oreilly.com/catalog/errata.csp?isbn=9781491914397* for release details.

978-1-491-91439-7

[LSI]

This book is dedicated to my 7th grade teacher who said that being a professional wrestler was not a career I could use for our "Life Plan" project, so instead I chose being an author. While it's not my full-time job, it still kind of came true...

Table of Contents

Part II. Working with Data

Part III. Code Architecture

Part IV.   A Practical Example

Preface

In today's society, websites are about giving people information quickly and effectively. Gone are the days of people waiting for websites to load. Enter single-page web designs and websites that work on your computer or your phone.

This book will bring three extremely useful technologies together to demonstrate how you can build a website that will work on many modern devices without writing specific code for each device.

ASP.NET MVC 5 will be used to build sophisticated web applications (the controller), interact with a database (the model), and dynamically render HTML (the view).

Bootstrap will be used to build sleek and responsive views that render on a variety of modern devices. Bootstrap provides a set of custom components that makes it easy to build an incredible user experience with easy-to-implement HTML, CSS, and JavaScript.

Knockout.js will bring these technologies together by enhancing the responsive web design with snappy client-side interactions driven by the server-side web application.

Why These Technologies?

That's a good question. If you have previous web development experience, it's easy to think that you don't need help, and that you can write your own HTML and CSS to create sleek and responsive web pages. I have more than 10 years of experience and since I was introduced to Bootstrap a few years ago, I've barely written any CSS.

Bootstrap provides two big advantages:

- The developers have taken the time to write and organize the CSS that is used repetitively to solve problems like creating a menu, making the menu stay at the top, allowing the menu to contain a search bar, etc. All of these things can be done with CSS, but it takes time! When you first write the code to do these things, there is a lot of small tweaking to get the alignment perfect. With Bootstrap, you don't need to worry about it because it has already been done.

- Not only have you saved time by not writing a lot of CSS to create your responsive website, but the developers of Bootstrap have *tested* all of the components in a variety of web browsers! This is really important because there are many subtle differences between each browser. For example, where only a little CSS tweak is needed for Internet Explorer, the same CSS might mess up Chrome. Because of Bootstrap, you can be confident that your website will work on a variety of browsers with just a little bit of effort on your part. This will allow you to focus your time on building a bigger, better, and more sophisticated project!

Knockout.js is a JavaScript library built on the MVVM (Model-View-ViewModel) architecture pattern. The defining factor of this pattern is to bind your data to a view through a ViewModel. This is extremely useful when building dynamic, responsive web applications because Knockout provides sophisticated logic to update your user interface automatically, based on user interaction.

Once again, this logic can be accomplished with JavaScript, but it takes a long time to write. As you'll see throughout this book, accomplishing it with Knockout.js takes very little time! And just like Bootstrap, these features are thoroughly tested in a variety of browsers, giving you a lot of confidence that your web application will work in any of the supported browsers.

The final piece of the web development puzzle is server-side technology that allows data persistence to and from a database, and the ability to write complex and well-structured business logic and to create intelligent HTML views that mix a combination of static and dynamic data together. ASP.NET MVC has progressed into a technology leader since its official version 1 release in March 2009. Now in its fifth iteration, it has become extremely powerful with many useful features available with just a few keystrokes.

Putting these three technologies together makes the development of complex, dynamic, and responsive web applications very rapid, where all of the heavy lifting is done for you. This book will demonstrate that and teach you ways to make your projects very well organized and easy to maintain.

What Is a Web Developer?

Recently, I was asked by a colleague, "Jamie, I'm thinking of switching careers and want to become a web developer. What do you think I need to learn?"

The colleague in question has great knowledge of several different programming languages (including C#). I quickly started to put a response together about learning MVC because his knowledge would transfer quite easily. I continued thinking that he'll also want to learn HTML, CSS, and JavaScript. And that got me thinking—a web developer doesn't just focus on one thing; we are more like a Jack-of-all-trades with a bit of knowledge of everything.

There are already countless books on learning MVC; however, they only focus on one aspect of web development. They teach you to save and retrieve information from a database, send emails to users, create a web application that lets users register and log in, etc. What these books don't do is teach you how to build forms that work on mobile devices or tablets that contain sleek user interfaces, use custom components that replace boring radio buttons, and so on.

Being a web developer involves all of these things and more. The goal of this book is not just to teach you to build a form that saves data to a database. Instead, we will build forms that use toggle buttons, modals, and popovers to create user interfaces that are easy to use, responsive, and dynamic all at once!

Who Is This Book For?

This book is for web developers, or for those who want to become one. It assumes that you have previous development experience with at least one programming language.

If you are a beginner, I would suggest you read this book from start to finish because many of the examples will build upon previous examples and, more importantly, topics discussed in previous chapters. More adventurous readers are free to jump from section to section for something of particular interest. Keep in mind that when examples extend previous ones, some may merely reference the earlier example to avoid redundant code listings where applicable.

The examples in this book will contain a mix of C#, HTML, CSS, and JavaScript. By the end of this book, you will be able to build incredibly sleek, dynamic, and responsive web applications rapidly by leveraging the capabilities of MVC 5, Bootstrap, and Knockout.js.

The book is separated into four parts. Part one provides an introduction to the three technologies used in the book. Part two demonstrates how to implement CRUD (Create-Read-Update-Delete) with the data being stored and read from a database. Part three dives into some more advanced C# and MVC features to help you organize and maintain your web applications. The final part demonstrates how to build a shopping cart from start to finish. The shopping cart will leverage many features of all three technologies, demonstrating how they interact with each other to create a sleek, dynamic, and responsive web application.

Getting Started

There are many different Integrated Development Environments (IDEs) to choose from that provide many useful shortcuts and code hints. I recommend using Visual Studio because it contains the best support for writing and building web applications using ASP.NET's MVC 5.

If it is not already installed, begin by visiting Microsoft's official MVC 5 website (*http://www.asp.net/mvc/mvc5*). Near the top of this website is a link to download and install a free version of Visual Studio Express 2013 that contains the templates to create MVC 5 web applications.

All of the examples in this book will assume that Visual Studio is being used when referencing elements within the IDE.

Conventions Used in This Book

The following typographical conventions are used in this book:

Italic
> Indicates new terms, URLs, email addresses, filenames, and file extensions.

`Constant width`
> Used for program listings, as well as within paragraphs to refer to program elements such as variable or function names, databases, data types, environment variables, statements, and keywords.

`Constant width bold`
> Shows commands or other text that should be typed literally by the user.

`Constant width italic`
> Shows text that should be replaced with user-supplied values or by values determined by context.

> This element signifies a tip or suggestion.

> This element signifies a general note.

This element indicates a warning or caution.

Using Code Examples

Supplemental material (code examples, exercises, etc.) is available for download at *https://github.com/oreillymedia/ASP_NET-MVC-5-with-Bootstrap-and-Knockout_js*.

This book is here to help you get your job done. In general, if example code is offered with this book, you may use it in your programs and documentation. You do not need to contact us for permission unless you're reproducing a significant portion of the code. For example, writing a program that uses several chunks of code from this book does not require permission. Selling or distributing a CD-ROM of examples from O'Reilly books does require permission. Answering a question by citing this book and quoting example code does not require permission. Incorporating a significant amount of example code from this book into your product's documentation does require permission.

We appreciate, but do not require, attribution. An attribution usually includes the title, author, publisher, and ISBN. For example: "*ASP.NET MVC 5 with Bootstrap and Knockout.js* by Jamie Munro (O'Reilly). Copyright 2015 Jamie Munro, 978-1-491-91439-7."

If you feel your use of code examples falls outside fair use or the permission given above, feel free to contact us at *permissions@oreilly.com*.

Safari® Books Online

 *Safari Books Online* is an on-demand digital library that delivers expert content in both book and video form from the world's leading authors in technology and business.

Technology professionals, software developers, web designers, and business and creative professionals use Safari Books Online as their primary resource for research, problem solving, learning, and certification training.

Safari Books Online offers a range of plans and pricing for enterprise, government, education, and individuals.

Members have access to thousands of books, training videos, and prepublication manuscripts in one fully searchable database from publishers like O'Reilly Media, Prentice Hall Professional, Addison-Wesley Professional, Microsoft Press, Sams, Que, Peachpit Press, Focal Press, Cisco Press, John Wiley & Sons, Syngress, Morgan Kaufmann, IBM Redbooks, Packt, Adobe Press, FT Press, Apress, Manning, New Riders, McGraw-Hill, Jones & Bartlett, Course Technology, and hundreds more. For more information about Safari Books Online, please visit us online.

How to Contact Us

Please address comments and questions concerning this book to the publisher:

> O'Reilly Media, Inc.
> 1005 Gravenstein Highway North
> Sebastopol, CA 95472
> 800-998-9938 (in the United States or Canada)
> 707-829-0515 (international or local)
> 707-829-0104 (fax)

We have a web page for this book, where we list errata, examples, and any additional information. You can access this page at *http://bit.ly/aspnet-mvc5*.

To comment or ask technical questions about this book, send email to *bookquestions@oreilly.com*.

For more information about our books, courses, conferences, and news, see our website at http://www.oreilly.com.

Find us on Facebook: *http://facebook.com/oreilly*.

Follow us on Twitter: *http://twitter.com/oreillymedia*.

Watch us on YouTube: *http://www.youtube.com/oreillymedia*.

Acknowledgements

This book was immensely challenging to write! I would not have been able to finish it if I didn't have an incredible support team around me, starting first and foremost with my wife, Shannon. Your unrelenting strength in caring for our children while I locked myself in a room to work is the only reason this book is done.

Next on the support team come a couple of former coworkers. Eric, you definitely provided the inspiration for why this book is required. Matt, your feedback during the technical review and the process for ensuring that the examples and explanations were clear and concise has gone along way toward making this book that much better.

Even though Mike wasn't part of this book, I always feel like I need to send out a special acknowledgement to him. Thanks, Mike, for putting up with my grumbling about how this project was never going to be finished. Your ability to help me procrastinate is second to none!

I think a special shout-out is required to my current (and former) coworkers at Fuse-bill. Without you guys, I would not have been working with MVC, Bootstrap, and Knockout.js every day for the past two years. As a team, I feel like we have learned so much about each technology and how to use them to their maximum capabilities.

A final shout-out goes to the entire team at O'Reilly. Thank you for providing me this opportunity to share my knowledge with the community. Kim, you did a fantastic job ensuring that my technical explanations are easy to follow without losing the important details in the mix.

PART I

Getting Started

CHAPTER 1

Introduction to MVC

MVC is an architecture pattern that stands for Model-View-Controller. My definition of MVC is summarized as follows:

- The model manages the data for the application. Each model commonly represents one or more tables within a database.
- The view contains the visual representation of the application. In websites, this is commonly achieved with HTML, CSS, and JavaScript.
- The controller is the middleman between the model and the view. A typical controller would request data from the model and pass it to the view for use in displaying the data. When saving data, it would be the opposite. It would receive data from the view and pass it to the model to save it.

ASP.NET MVC 5 is a framework that implements the Model-View-Controller (MVC) architecture pattern.

The term *MVC* will be mentioned repeatedly throughout this book. In most scenarios, I will be referring to the MVC framework that implements the MVC pattern.

Creating Your First Project

Visual Studio offers a variety of templates that help you start your project. This book will focus on two specific templates: MVC and Web API.

The MVC template allows the creation of web applications that use the Model-View-Controller architecture pattern. This will be discussed in more detail throughout this book.

The Web API template allows for the creation of RESTful web applications. REST is another type of software architecture pattern that is commonly used for creating APIs or client-server applications. Web API is easily integrated into the MVC architecture pattern, which will allow reuse between your MVC and Web API projects, as will be demonstrated later in this book.

For this first example, I will focus on the MVC template. From the Visual Studio Start Page or from the File Menu, select the New Project option. As you can see, there are many different types of projects that you can create. Under the Templates menu, expand the Visual C# menu. From here, select the Web option. In my default installation, I have only one option of an ASP.NET Web Application. Select this and enter a project name in the space provided. I have chosen BootstrapIntroduction.

Once you have selected a project name, click the OK button. You are now presented with several different Web templates. Select the MVC template. Once the MVC template is selected, you will notice additional options to include Web API and to include a Unit Test project. For this example, I will leave them unselected.

With the MVC template, there are also four different Authentication options:

No Authentication
> All pages of your website will be publicly available.

Individual User Accounts
> With this option, your web application will allow users to register and log in by creating their own username and password. It also provides several different Social Login options, including Facebook, Twitter, Google, and Microsoft Account. Any of the various scenarios will store the information in the membership database that is automatically created.

Organizational Accounts
> With this option, your web application will integrate with Active Directory, Microsoft Azure Active Directory, or Office 365 to secure pages within your application.

Windows Authentication
> With this option, your web application is secured using the Windows Authentication IIS module. This is common for intranet applications where all of the user accounts exist on the web server hosting the application.

For the purposes of this example, I have changed it to No Authentication, as shown in Figure 1-1.

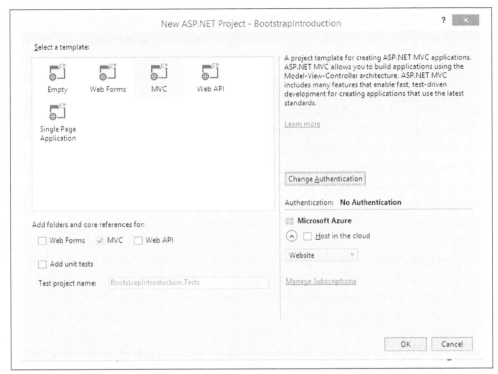

Figure 1-1. Project creation

When you are ready, click OK to complete the project creation. Depending on the speed of your computer, this may take one or two minutes while the project is being configured and preloaded with many useful files and folders to help you get started.

Once completed, you will be able to select *Start Debugging* from the *Debug* menu. This will launch your new web application in your default web browser.

When you look at the folders, you will notice that each role in MVC has its own folder. The *Views* folder commonly contains a subfolder that matches the Controller name because it typically contains more than one view to allow easy organization of your files.

If you expand the *Views* folder, you will see two subfolders: *Home* and *Shared*. The *Home* folder matches the HomeController that exists in the *Controllers* folder. The *Shared* folder is used for views that contain common code between other views.

This includes layouts or partial views. Layouts are special views that contain the reusable view on each page. A partial view is a reusable view that contains a subset of data that can be included in one or more pages.

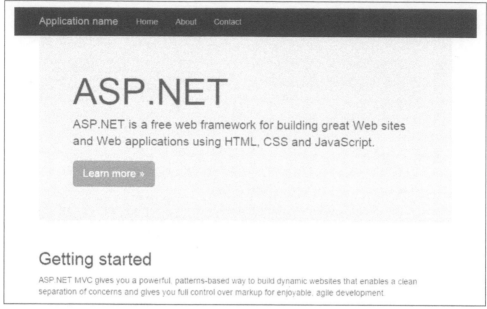

Figure 1-2. The default website

Figure 1-2 is a screenshot of the default website that is created with a new MVC project. The menu contains three links: Home, About, and Contact. Let's keep those in mind as we begin exploring the code.

Examining the HomeController

Let's start by looking at the controller. Under the *Controllers* folder is a file called *HomeController.cs*, and it should look like Example 1-1.

Example 1-1. HomeController.cs

```
using System;
using System.Collections.Generic;
using System.Linq;
using System.Web;
using System.Web.Mvc;

namespace BootstrapIntroduction.Controllers
{
  public class HomeController : Controller
  {
    public ActionResult Index()
    {
      return View();
    }
```

```
    public ActionResult About()
    {
      ViewBag.Message = "Your application description page.";

      return View();
    }

    public ActionResult Contact()
    {
      ViewBag.Message = "Your contact page.";

      return View();
    }
  }
}
```

The `HomeController` is a class that contains three methods: `Index`, `About`, and `Con` `tact`. In MVC terms, these are commonly referred to as *actions*. An action named `Index` is usually the main entry point for a controller. Notice how each action matches the names of the links that were created with the exception of `Home`, because that refers to the `Index` action.

All controllers in an MVC application will extend the base `Controller` class. Each method in the class returns a type called `ActionResult`. In most scenarios, all of your actions will return this. We will explore other return types in future examples.

The `About` and `Contact` actions also introduce the `ViewBag` property of the `Control` `ler` class. This property allows you to dynamically pass data to your view. Example 1-2 will demonstrate how it is used within the view.

The ViewBag

The `ViewBag` property allows you to share data between your controllers and your views. This variable is defined as a dynamic type and contains no predefined properties, which allows you to specify any name for your property and have it contain any type of data.

Finally, each action is returned with a call to the `View` function. This method exists in the `Controller` class that all controllers extend. It loads the view and executes the Razor code contained within your *.cshtml* file. In Example 1-1, no parameters are passed into the function, which means that, by default, MVC will look for a view with the same name as the function.

Examining the Views

When you expand the *Views* folder, there is a subfolder called *Home*. This contains three files: *About.cshtml*, *Contact.cshtml*, and *Index.cshtml*. Each file is named after its action name in the controller. The extension *.cshtml* stands for C# HTML. These views allow for Razor (*http://bit.ly/razor-syntax*)syntax, which is a combination of HTML mixed with C#. This provides the ability to implement common coding techniques like conditional statements, loops, and outputting of dynamic data (such as the ViewBag property previously mentioned).

Example 1-2 is the default About page that is created with the project. Elements that use Razor begin with the @ symbol. When it is combined with a curly brace ({), this allows for multiline C# code. In this example, it is setting the page title in the ViewBag property to "About". The Title property on the ViewBag is commonly used in the shared layout to set the title of the page that your browser shows. This example also displays it within an h2 tag.

Example 1-2. About.cshtml

```
@{
  ViewBag.Title = "About";
}
<h2>@ViewBag.Title.</h2>
<h3>@ViewBag.Message</h3>

<p>Use this area to provide additional information.</p>
```

In addition to the Title property, the Message property in the ViewBag is shown in an h3 tag. As you recall, this was set in the controller action for the About and Con tact methods.

This is a great example of how Razor is interjected with standard HTML to produce dynamic content when rendered to a browser.

You may notice that when you browse the About page there is a lot more HTML than just these few elements. This is accomplished with a shared layout. By default, all views are placed within a default template, which is under the other folder within *Views* called *Shared*. If you expand this folder, you will see the *_Layout.cshtml* file, as shown in Example 1-3.

Example 1-3. _Layout.cshtml

```
<!DOCTYPE html>
<html>
<head>
  <meta charset="utf-8" />
```

```
    <meta name="viewport" content="width=device-width, initial-scale=1.0">
    <title>@ViewBag.Title - My ASP.NET Application</title>
    @Styles.Render("~/Content/css")
    @Scripts.Render("~/bundles/modernizr")
</head>
<body>
    <div class="navbar navbar-inverse navbar-fixed-top">
        <div class="container">
            <div class="navbar-header">
                <button type="button" class="navbar-toggle" data-toggle="collapse"
                        data-target=".navbar-collapse">
                    <span class="icon-bar"></span>
                    <span class="icon-bar"></span>
                    <span class="icon-bar"></span>
                </button>
                @Html.ActionLink("Application name", "Index", "Home",
                        new { area = "" }, new { @class = "navbar-brand" })
            </div>
            <div class="navbar-collapse collapse">
                <ul class="nav navbar-nav">
                    <li>@Html.ActionLink("Home", "Index", "Home")</li>
                    <li>@Html.ActionLink("About", "About", "Home")</li>
                    <li>@Html.ActionLink("Contact", "Contact", "Home")</li>
                </ul>
            </div>
        </div>
    </div>
    <div class="container body-content">
        @RenderBody()
        <hr />
        <footer>
            <p>&copy; @DateTime.Now.Year - My ASP.NET Application</p>
        </footer>
    </div>

    @Scripts.Render("~/bundles/jquery")
    @Scripts.Render("~/bundles/bootstrap")
    @RenderSection("scripts", required: false)
</body>
</html>
```

The default layout contains the reusable HTML that appears on every page within the
site (elements such as the page title, header, footer, CSS, JavaScript, etc.).

The view that is being rendered is inserted into this layout when the function Render
Body is called via Razor code.

There are a lot of other things happening in this shared layout. It is using several
helper classes provided by the MVC framework, such as the HtmlHelper (*http://bit.ly/
htmlhelper*)class to create links, the Scripts (*http://bit.ly/scripts-render*) class to include
JavaScript files, the Styles (*http://bit.ly/styles-render*) class to include CSS files, and Ren

der`Section` to allow your views to mark specific content to be inserted in a specific spot in the shared layout. This will be shown in Chapter 2.

Understanding the URL Structure

When you launched the default website, three links were created:

- The Home link. This took you to the root of the site (/).
- The About link. This took you to */Home/About*.
- The Contact link. This took you to */Home/Contact*.

These links work because when an MVC project is first created, a default route is configured to make them work. Routes allow your website to tell MVC how it should map a URL to a specific controller and action within your project.

Routes are configured in the *App_Start/RouteConfig.cs* file. Example 1-4 shows the default route that is configured with a new MVC project.

Example 1-4. Default route

```
routes.MapRoute(
  name: "Default",
  url: "{controller}/{action}/{id}",
  defaults: new { controller = "Home", action = "Index", id = UrlParameter.Optional }
);
```

Three important things are defined in this route config:

- A name. Each route must have a unique name.
- The URL. This is a relative URL after the website's domain name. The URL can contain a mix of static text and variables.
- Default configuration. If any of the variables in the URL are not provided, defaults may be set for them.

If we reanalyze the links mentioned earlier, they work because:

- When we go to / the URL contains no controller, action, or ID. The defaults that are set indicate that it will go to the `HomeController`, the `Index` action, and the ID does not need to exist.
- When we go to */Home/About* and */Home/Contact*, no defaults are used because both the controller and action are specified in the URL.

In fact, the Home link can also be accessed via */Home* and */Home/Index* as well. However, when URLs are created within a view, MVC picks the shortest, most accurate URL, e.g., just /.

With this route, you can create a new controller and/or action, and it can automatically be accessed by its name and action name.

Summary

If you are new to MVC, this chapter might feel overwhelming. The predefined MVC templates in Visual Studio are quite extensive and provide developers with a large head start in their projects.

Because of this, it's difficult to cover every detail of what gets created. In this introductory chapter, I have covered many of the core features that will get you started.

There are many more details to cover with Models-Views-Controllers. As this book progresses and covers more advanced topics, they will be explored thoroughly in those chapters.

CHAPTER 2

Introduction to Bootstrap

Bootstrap is an HTML, CSS, and JavaScript framework that creates consistent-looking, responsive websites. Bootstrap is automatically installed with MVC 5 applications and is immediately seen in action within the default layout that was created in Chapter 1. Through the use of basic HTML styled with specific CSS classes, it's easy to create very nice-looking web pages.

This chapter will explore the many common components of Bootstrap, such as menus, buttons, and alerts. You can visit the Bootstrap Components (*http://getboot strap.com/components/*)listing for a more in-depth overview of the plethora of components that have been created. Some of the more complex components that require a combination of JavaScript, HTML, and CSS will be covered in future chapters when they are integrated with Knockout.js.

Examining the Default Menu

The project that we created in Chapter 1 contains an example of one of Bootstrap's menus with a responsive design. Let's explore its structure now. It is contained in *Views/Shared/_Layout.cshtml*. When this menu is rendered in a browser, it looks like Figure 2-1.

Figure 2-1. The default menu

Defining a menu with Bootstrap requires a div tag with the class of navbar as shown in Example 2-1.

Example 2-1. Starting the menu

```
<div class="navbar navbar-inverse navbar-fixed-top">
</div>
```

This example also specifies two additional classes: navbar-inverse and navbar-fixed-top. By specifying the navbar-inverse class, Bootstrap will make the menu the inverse of the default coloring. With the default theme, that means black instead of transparent. The navbar-fixed-top class will cause the menu to always remain fixed at the top of the page, meaning if the content allows you to scroll down, the menu will remain visible at the top.

The list of navigational elements are commonly defined in a list tag (ul) attributed with a class called nav. Each navigation element is then defined in its own list item or li tag as shown in Example 2-2.

Example 2-2. Defining the menu links

```
<div class="navbar navbar-inverse navbar-fixed-top">
  <div class="navbar-collapse collapse">
    <ul class="nav navbar-nav">
      <li>@Html.ActionLink("Home", "Index", "Home")</li>
      <li>@Html.ActionLink("About", "About", "Home")</li>
      <li>@Html.ActionLink("Contact", "Contact", "Home")</li>
    </ul>
  </div>
</div>
```

As I've mentioned, Bootstrap provides a responsive web layout. This means when the website is viewed in a browser with a different screen resolution, the page will adjust automatically.

As shown in Example 2-2, just above the ul tag that defines the three main links is a div with the class navbar-collapse. When this page is viewed on a small device (or you resize your browser), the menu will automatically collapse to ensure that the menu fits properly in the provided resolution. This example adds a second class to the div of collapse, which will make the menu completely hidden if it won't fit on a single line.

Of course, this wouldn't provide very good usability, and this example has already thought of that. It adds a little button on the right-hand side that, when clicked, toggles the display of the three buttons as shown in Figure 2-2.

Figure 2-2. A collapsed menu

The button to show and hide the menu is created with several different attributes, so when clicked, the menu is shown as demonstrated in Example 2-3.

Example 2-3. Button for collapsed menu

```
<div class="navbar navbar-inverse navbar-fixed-top">
  <div class="container">
    <div class="navbar-header">
      <button type="button" class="navbar-toggle" data-toggle="collapse"
              data-target=".navbar-collapse">
        <span class="icon-bar"></span>
        <span class="icon-bar"></span>
        <span class="icon-bar"></span>
      </button>
      @Html.ActionLink("Application name", "Index", "Home",
              new { area = "" }, new { @class = "navbar-brand" })
    </div>
    <div class="navbar-collapse collapse">
      <ul class="nav navbar-nav">
        <li>@Html.ActionLink("Home", "Index", "Home")</li>
        <li>@Html.ActionLink("About", "About", "Home")</li>
        <li>@Html.ActionLink("Contact", "Contact", "Home")</li>
      </ul>
    </div>
  </div>
</div>
```

Previously, everything was accomplished via CSS classes on HTML elements. The collapse button introduces data attributes that are used in the JavaScript provided by Bootstrap. The `data-toggle` attribute with a value of `collapse` indicates that it should remain invisible until the menu requires collapsing. The `data-target` attribute indicates which element that is currently being hidden should be displayed (or hidden) when the button is clicked; in this case, it is `.navbar-collapse`. The button is styled and placed on the right-hand side by the class `navbar-toggle`.

The Data Target

Notice that in Example 2-3 the class `navbar-collapse` is prefixed with a period (.). The value within the attribute is used within a jQuery selector to find the element and show or hide it. If the menu were identified by an ID, it would require a hash tag (#) prefix before the ID assigned to it.

Now enter the power of the many different Bootstrap components. In Example 2-2, the `ul` tag contains a secondary class of `navbar-nav`. Bootstrap provides several different classes that can create a variety of different-looking menus.

If you replace the `navbar-nav` class with `nav-pills`, a different-looking menu is displayed. I also added the class `active` to the first `li` item (see Example 2-4).

Example 2-4. Changing to pills stylized menu

```
<ul class="nav nav-pills">
  <li class="active">@Html.ActionLink("Home", "Index", "Home")</li>
  <li>@Html.ActionLink("About", "About", "Home")</li>
  <li>@Html.ActionLink("Contact", "Contact", "Home")</li>
</ul>
```

When rendered, it looks slightly different as shown in Figure 2-3.

Figure 2-3. A pill menu

A Menu with Drop-Downs and a Search Box

The default menu that was created by MVC is pretty comprehensive. However, Bootstrap provides a lot more functionality that can be implemented in a menu. This next example will explore a more complex menu that will contain a mix of navigation elements with and without drop-downs, as well as a search box with a button.

Just like the default menu, starting a new menu requires the `navbar` class as shown in Example 2-5. This time, it will use the default colors (instead of the inverse), and it won't be fixed to the top.

Example 2-5. Starting the menu

```
<nav class="navbar navbar-default" role="navigation">

</nav>
```

The next thing that is required is the "branding" of the application as shown in Example 2-6. It will be contained in a separate element with the button to show the menu when it's collapsed, to ensure that it is grouped together when the resolution is too small to show the full menu.

Example 2-6. Menu with branding

```
<nav class="navbar navbar-default" role="navigation">
  <div class="navbar-header">
    <button type="button" class="navbar-toggle collapsed" data-toggle="collapse"
        data-target=".navbar-collapse">
      <span class="sr-only">Toggle navigation</span>
      <span class="icon-bar"></span>
      <span class="icon-bar"></span>
      <span class="icon-bar"></span>
    </button>
    <a class="navbar-brand" href="@Url.Action("Index", "Home")">Application name</a>
  </div>
</nav>
```

This contains the same button as shown in the Figure 2-2 that will be displayed when the menu is collapsed. Notice that the links are defined differently. Previously, they were completely defined with Razor. However, the next links (in Example 2-7) require HTML within the link text, so it's better to have complete control over the `a` tag. It is still important to let MVC compile the URL for us, so it's using the `Url Helper` to build the link instead of the `HtmlHelper`.

Next up are the three links to Home, About, and Contact as shown in Example 2-7. About and Contact have been updated to include drop-down links to fictitious sub-pages. The About drop-down even contains a nice divider between the second and third link.

Example 2-7. Drop-down menus

```
<nav class="navbar navbar-default" role="navigation">
  <div class="navbar-header">
    <button type="button" class="navbar-toggle collapsed" data-toggle="collapse"
        data-target=".navbar-collapse">
      <span class="sr-only">Toggle navigation</span>
      <span class="icon-bar"></span>
      <span class="icon-bar"></span>
      <span class="icon-bar"></span>
    </button>
    <a class="navbar-brand" href="@Url.Action("Index", "Home")">Application name</a>
  </div>
  <div class="collapse navbar-collapse">
    <ul class="nav navbar-nav">
      <li class="active"><a href="@Url.Action("Index", "Home")">Home</a></li>
```

```
          <li class="dropdown">
            <a href="@Url.Action("About", "Home")" class="dropdown-toggle"
                    data-toggle="dropdown">About <span class="caret"></span></a>
            <ul class="dropdown-menu" role="menu">
              <li><a href="#">The Executive Team</a></li>
              <li><a href="#">Who We Are</a></li>
              <li class="divider"></li>
              <li><a href="#">Jobs</a></li>
            </ul>
          </li>
          <li class="dropdown">
            <a href="@Url.Action("Contact", "Home")" class="dropdown-toggle"
                    data-toggle="dropdown">Contact <span class="caret"></span></a>
            <ul class="dropdown-menu" role="menu">
              <li><a href="#">By Mail</a></li>
              <li><a href="#">By E-mail</a></li>
            </ul>
          </li>
        </ul>
      </div>
</nav>
```

The li elements for drop-downs are tagged with the dropdown class. The link is then affixed with the dropdown-toggle class and the data-toggle of dropdown. Beneath the link is an unordered list with each link in a li tag. Inside the About drop-down is an empty li tag that contains the class divider.

To complete this menu, a search form will be created and aligned to the right side of the menu as shown in Example 2-8.

Example 2-8. The search form

```
<nav class="navbar navbar-default" role="navigation">
  <div class="navbar-header">
    <button type="button" class="navbar-toggle collapsed" data-toggle="collapse"
          data-target=".navbar-collapse">
      <span class="sr-only">Toggle navigation</span>
      <span class="icon-bar"></span>
      <span class="icon-bar"></span>
      <span class="icon-bar"></span>
    </button>
    <a class="navbar-brand" href="@Url.Action("Index", "Home")">Application name</a>
  </div>
  <div class="collapse navbar-collapse">
    <ul class="nav navbar-nav">
      <li class="active"><a href="@Url.Action("Index", "Home")">Home</a></li>
      <li class="dropdown">
        <a href="@Url.Action("About", "Home")" class="dropdown-toggle"
                data-toggle="dropdown">About <span class="caret"></span></a>
        <ul class="dropdown-menu" role="menu">
          <li><a href="#">The Executive Team</a></li>
```

```
        <li><a href="#">Who We Are</a></li>
        <li class="divider"></li>
        <li><a href="#">Jobs</a></li>
      </ul>
    </li>
    <li class="dropdown">
      <a href="@Url.Action("Contact", "Home")" class="dropdown-toggle"
               data-toggle="dropdown">Contact <span class="caret"></span></a>
      <ul class="dropdown-menu" role="menu">
        <li><a href="#">By Mail</a></li>
        <li><a href="#">By E-mail</a></li>
      </ul>
    </li>
  </ul>
  <form class="navbar-form navbar-right" role="search">
    <div class="form-group">
      <input type="text" class="form-control" placeholder="Search">
    </div>
    <button type="submit" class="btn btn-default">Submit</button>
  </form>
  </div>
</nav>
```

The final menu looks (in my opinion) really slick (shown in Figure 2-4) with an inline search form aligned to the far right of the menu.

Figure 2-4. The final menu

The inline form and alignment are accomplished by adding the `navbar-form` and `navbar-right` classes to the `form` tag as shown in Example 2-8.

Buttons

Another very common thing on any website are buttons. Bootstrap has built six different themed buttons. They are named and look as shown in Figure 2-5.

Figure 2-5. The six button styles

Note the names: Default, Primary, Success, Info, Warning, and Danger. These are used in several other components as well, and the colors remain consistent between them. Example 2-9 demonstrates how to create the buttons shown in Figure 2-5.

Example 2-9. Making the buttons

```
<button type="button" class="btn btn-default">Default</button>
<button type="button" class="btn btn-primary">Primary</button>
<button type="button" class="btn btn-success">Success</button>
<button type="button" class="btn btn-info">Info</button>
<button type="button" class="btn btn-warning">Warning</button>
<button type="button" class="btn btn-danger">Danger</button>
```

Each button is created by specifying two classes. The first is btn, and it is consistent between all of the buttons. Next is a class that begins with btn- and finishes with the type of button being created, e.g., success or danger.

These classes are not limited to only HTML button tags. They can be applied with links or submit buttons as well.

Just like the menu created earlier, buttons can be created with drop-downs as well. This provides a nice solution when you require a selection from the user where multiple options are available.

Another nice feature of buttons is that you can group them together. Example 2-10 will explore these options mixed together.

Example 2-10. Button group with drop-down

```
<div class="btn-group">
  <button type="button" class="btn btn-default">Default</button>
  <button type="button" class="btn btn-primary">Primary</button>
  <button type="button" class="btn btn-success">Success</button>
  <button type="button" class="btn btn-success dropdown-toggle"
   data-toggle="dropdown">
    <span class="caret"></span>
  </button>
  <ul class="dropdown-menu" role="menu">
    <li><a href="#">Option 1</a></li>
    <li><a href="#">Option 2</a></li>
  </ul>
</div>
```

The result of this button group looks like Figure 2-6.

Figure 2-6. A button group

The drop-down in the button is accomplished identically to the menu—the list of options are contained within a ul tag, and each option is contained within a li tag. The drop-down icon is its own button that contains a span tag with caret as the class name. Because the buttons are contained within a div with class btn-group, they are tightly coupled together. This gives the appearance that the button with "Success" and the drop-down icon are the same button, even though it is implemented with a two-button tags.

Alerts

Prior to using Bootstrap, I didn't often deal with alert messages because I felt the implementation effort exceeded the value they provided. Bootstrap definitely alleviates this concern.

Figure 2-7 demonstrates the four different types of alert messages. Alert messages optionally include the ability to be dismissed with the "x" in the right corner, which allows users to hide the message once they have read it.

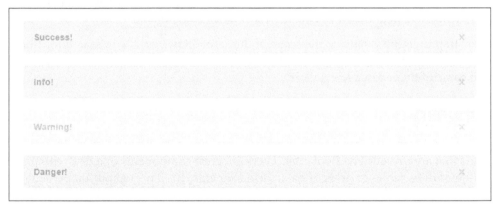

Figure 2-7. Alert messages

Example 2-11. Dismissible alert messages

```
<div class="alert alert-success alert-dismissible" role="alert">
  <button type="button" class="close" data-dismiss="alert">
      <span aria-hidden="true">&times;</span><span class="sr-only">Close</span>
    </button>
  <strong>Success!</strong>
</div>
```

Example 2-11 demonstrates that creating an alert is quite similar to creating buttons when dealing with the styling. A success button would contain two classes: btn and btn-success. Alerts work the same way, replacing btn with alert.

Note that, by default, alerts do not support the `default` and `primary` classes that buttons support.

Like buttons, if I wanted to create a warning alert, or a danger alert I would replace `alert-success` with `alert-warning` or `alert-danger`, respectively.

A third class is added to this alert message: `alert-dismissible`. Inside the `div` tag is a button with a class of `close` and an attribute `data-dismiss` with the value `alert`. This combination will allow the Bootstrap CSS and JavaScript to stylize and make the alert box disappear when the user clicks the x in the top-right corner.

Themes

As shown when creating buttons and alert boxes, Bootstrap leverages common class names that are converted to a consistent color theme. If you are adventurous, you can edit any of the coloring, spacing, and so on by editing the Bootstrap CSS. In MVC, the file is located in the *Content* directory and appropriately named *bootstrap.css*.

Because of Bootstrap's consistent nature, there are hundreds of different themes that people have created to further enhance the built-in components.

Bootstrap theming is outside the scope of this book; however, if you search for Bootstrap themes on Google, you will find many different types. Many of them are free and some of them cost a few dollars.

Summary

The examples in this chapter barely scratch the surface of the more than 70 components that are provided by Bootstrap. There are great components that deal with paginating of data, tables or grids of data, form elements, etc. Throughout the remainder of this book, I will explore a variety of these components while integrating them with MVC.

This chapter contains example HTML for multiple menus, buttons, button groups, and alert messages that is barely more than 50 lines of code. If you were to create the same styling without Bootstrap, you would also need to write several hundred lines of CSS and accompanying JavaScript to make the drop-down menus and dismissible alert messages!

In my opinion, this makes using Bootstrap in all of my projects a no-brainer.

CHAPTER 3

Introduction to Knockout.js

Knockout.js is an open source JavaScript library that allows you to create dynamic and rich web applications. It is built with the Model-View-ViewModel (MVVM) pattern. Knockout makes it really simple to implement a complex user interface that responds to user interactions.

I like Knockout because it is one of the most lightweight JavaScript libraries available today. It also doesn't try to be an all-in-one framework. It serves a single purpose: data binding your ViewModel to your user interface.

Implementing Knockout involves three distinct things: a view that contains HTML and CSS elements that get data-bound to it, a ViewModel that contains the data to bind to the view, and telling Knockout to perform the data binding to the view with the ViewModel.

Installing Knockout.js

Knockout.js can be installed in one of two ways:

- Downloading the latest version from the Knockout downloads page (*http://knock outjs.com/downloads*).
- Installing Knockout via the NuGet Package Manager.

My preference is the NuGet Package Manager because it makes it easier to update to a new version if/when a newer version is available.

The NuGet Package Manager is integrated directly into Visual Studio and allows developers to easily install (or create their own) packages to install and manage third-party dependencies.

To install Knockout, perform the following operations:

1. Click the Tools menu.
2. Click the NuGet Package Manager submenu.
3. Click the NuGet Packages for Solution menu.
4. On the left, click Online if it is not already selected.
5. In the search box on the top right, type **knockoutjs**.
6. The first package is the Knockout framework. Click the Install button for this package (see Figure 3-1).
7. Next, choose which project to install it on. Assuming that you have just the one project, the default option of "All" is OK. If, in the future, you have multiple projects, be sure to select the project that contains your MVC application.
8. Once the package is installed, click the Close button on the NuGet Package Manager.

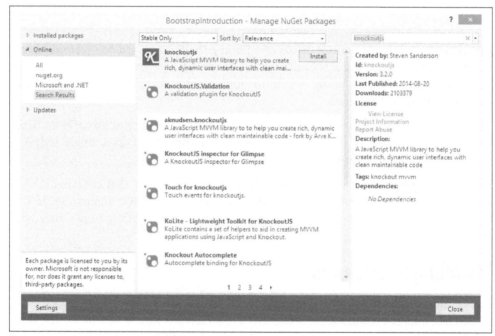

Figure 3-1. Installing the Knockout package

With the Knockout library downloaded and added to the project, it becomes a simple matter of including the script.

In the *Views/Shared/_Layout.cshtml* file, add the code from Example 3-1 just above the @RenderSection located just above the ending body tag (</body>).

Example 3-1. Including the Knockout library

```
<script src="~/Scripts/knockout-3.2.0.js" type="text/javascript"></script>
```

You may notice that right above this line there is Razor code that starts with @Scripts.Render. This is another way of including JavaScript files; however, it requires creating a JavaScript bundle. Bundling and minification of JavaScript files will be covered in Chapter 12.

NuGet Package Updates

If you reopen the NuGet Package Manager and select the Updates menu option on the left, you will see a long list of packages that require updating.

These packages were installed by default when the project was created through the Visual Studio template. Because the template uses fixed versions of the package and was created many months ago, it's possible that the referenced libraries have been updated.

Before beginning a new project, it's a great idea to update any packages that you will be using. Likewise, if there are dependencies that you will not be using, it's a good idea to remove them and clean up the included packages.

A Basic Example

Now that the Knockout library is installed, let's get right to an example of using it. Knockout works with ViewModels, which are comprised of JavaScript code that is executed by Knockout and bound to the view. Many different ViewModels will be created throughout this book.

Example 3-2 creates a new Razor view called *Basic.cshtml* and is placed inside the *Views/Home folder*.

Example 3-2. A basic ViewModel

```
@{
  ViewBag.Title = "Basic";
}

<h2>Hello <span data-bind="text: name"></span></h2>

@section Scripts {
<script>
  function ViewModel() {
    this.name = 'Eric McQuiggan';
  };

  var viewModel = new ViewModel();
  ko.applyBindings(viewModel);
</script>
}
```

I mentioned in the introduction that there are three important pieces that make Knockout work:

- HTML and CSS that contain elements that are data bound to it from the View-Model. This example is using a `span` tag that contains an HTML attribute called `data-bind` with the contents of `text: name`.
- The ViewModel that contains the properties and/or functions that are used in the data binding. In this example, it is a function called `ViewModel` that contains a single variable called `name` that is set to the value of `Eric McQuiggan`.
- The final piece is to tell Knockout to execute the bindings on the View with a specific ViewModel. In this example, the `ViewModel` function is instantiated like a class and stored in a variable called `viewModel`. This variable is then passed to the `ko.applyBindings` function, which takes the `name` variable from the View-Model and replaces the contents within the `span` tag with the contents of the variable.

@section Scripts

You might have noticed that the JavaScript was placed inside the following Razor code: `@section Scripts { }`. This is a good code practice within a view because inside the shared layout right below where the Knockout library was included in Example 3-1 is the `@RenderSection` of this section. When the view is executed, the Razor engine will extract the JavaScript and place it there when the view is rendered in the browser.

Before this example can be run, the `HomeController` must be updated to call the newly created view. Example 3-3 contains an updated controller with a new action that will render the view.

Example 3-3. Updated HomeController

```
using System;
using System.Collections.Generic;
using System.Linq;
using System.Web;
using System.Web.Mvc;

namespace BootstrapIntroduction.Controllers
{
  public class HomeController : Controller
  {
    public ActionResult Index()
    {
      return View();
```

```
    }

    public ActionResult About()
    {
      ViewBag.Message = "Your application description page.";

      return View();
    }

    public ActionResult Contact()
    {
      ViewBag.Message = "Your contact page.";

      return View();
    }

    public ActionResult Basic()
    {
      return View();
    }
  }
}
```

You can now debug the project by pressing the default shortcut key of F5. Visual Studio will compile your project and launch your default web browser with a URL that will look something like *http://localhost:50955/*. Adding *Home/Basic* to the end of the URL will display the newly created view and execute the Knockout code as shown in Figure 3-2.

Figure 3-2. Hello world example

What Is MVVM?

The *Model-View-ViewModel* (MVVM) design pattern is based largely on the Model-View-Controller (MVC) pattern. In fact, the MV is shared between them. It's the ViewModel that really separates the two.

MVVM was designed to implement (as shown in Figure 3-3) data binding between your ViewModel and your View. This is what Knockout does for you, and it does it very well. It is accomplished using some simple-to-implement HTML attributes and a JavaScript ViewModel as shown in Example 3-2.

The most important thing to remember when you are building ViewModels is that they should be organized to make it easy to represent how your View uses the data. This is an important distinction because Models in MVC are typically represented in how they are stored in the database.

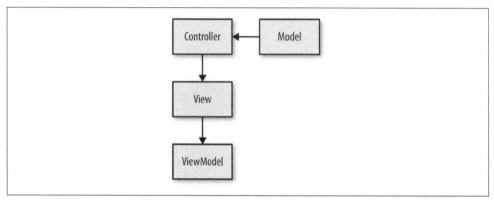

Figure 3-3. Understanding MVVM

The most common example of this is a name. As shown in Example 3-2, a single name variable contains both the first and last name of the person. However, if we were to collect a person's name with a form, I would separate it into two fields. If the name was left as two fields when used for display, it would require maintaining two variables and rendering them both on-screen instead of amalgamating them into a single variable representing the user's full name.

In this example, the Model (in MVC) would contain a first and last name, whereas the ViewModel would contain a single field created from the two fields.

Creating ViewModels

A ViewModel can be any type of JavaScript variable. Example 3-4 demonstrates this by replacing the ViewModel that was created in Example 3-2 with a simple JavaScript variable that contains the same property name.

Example 3-4. Another ViewModel

```
<script>
  var viewModel = {
    name: 'Eric McQuiggan'
```

```
  };

  ko.applyBindings(viewModel);
</script>
```

Running this example will output the same result as Figure 3-2. Typically, when I create ViewModels, I create simple or complex JavaScript classes that allow me to leverage an object-oriented style of programming (functions, properties, abstraction, etc.).

Object-Oriented Programming with JavaScript

JavaScript is a fully object-oriented programming (OOP) language based on prototyping. It doesn't contain class statements like C++, C#, or PHP; however, JavaScript functions can be used to simulate the same behavior.

It also offers full support of OOP language features such as namespaces, objects, properties, inheritance, abstraction, etc.

If you are new to JavaScript or object-oriented programming, the Mozilla Developer Network (MDN) offers a great introductory article (*http://mzl.la/1u0uge8*).

In the previous examples, the name property was hardcoded inside the ViewModel. It's more common that this data would be populated from the MVC application. Example 3-5 will create a new view called *Advanced.cshtml* and place it within the same *Views/Home* folder.

Example 3-5. ViewModel that accepts the name as input

```
@model BootstrapIntroduction.Models.Person
@{
  ViewBag.Title = "Advanced";
}

<h2>Hello <span data-bind="text: getName()"></span></h2>

@section Scripts {
  <script>
    function ViewModel(firstName, lastName) {
      var self = this;

      self.name = firstName + ' ' + lastName;

      self.getName = function () {
        return self.name;
      };
    };
```

```
    var viewModel = new ViewModel('@Model.FirstName', '@Model.LastName');
    ko.applyBindings(viewModel);
  </script>
}
```

Once again, executing Knockout requires three important steps:

1. HTML and CSS contain elements that are to be data bound from the ViewModel. Similar to Example 3-2, a span tag is used, but this time the text binding is calling the getName function in the ViewModel. This function is a wrapper to the name property.
2. The ViewModel that contains the variables and functions that will be bound to the HTML. Example 3-5 is slightly different from Example 3-2 because it accepts the first name and last name as variables in the constructor to the ViewModel. This is then concatenated and stored to the name property and accessed by the getName function.
3. And finally, the ViewModel is executed by Knockout when the ko.applyBind ings function is called with the ViewModel.

When the ViewModel is created, it is populating the name with Razor code to access the Model that is associated with this view (the person model). This will be set in Example 3-6 when the HomeController is updated. It's important that the Razor syntax is contained within quotes because when this is parsed by Razor, it will be rendered as JavaScript code. Because it is contained within quotes, it will be executed as a JavaScript string instead of a variable, which would cause an error because it doesn't exist.

Self = This

You may be wondering why the first line of my ViewModel is var self = this;. By creating a variable called self and assigning it the variable this, it provides me with a property that I can use inside methods of my class and easily reference other methods or properties in my class.

Before running this example, the HomeController must be updated to add a new function called Advanced (as shown in Example 3-6). This function creates a new Person model (shown in Example 3-7) and provides this object as a parameter to the View function. The data in this model is used by the view when the ViewModel is constructed in the JavaScript.

Example 3-6. Advanced function to be placed in HomeController

```
public ActionResult Advanced()
{
  var person = new Person
  {
    FirstName = "Eric",
    LastName = "McQuiggan"
  };

  return View(person);
}
```

And finally, a *Person.cs* file should be created inside of the *Models* folder that contains the code from Example 3-7.

Example 3-7. The Person model

```
namespace BootstrapIntroduction.Models
{
  public class Person
  {
    public string FirstName { get; set; }

    public string LastName { get; set; }
  }
}
```

Running this example will produce the same output as Figure 3-2.

Summary

This introduction to Knockout only demonstrated one type of data binding that Knockout supports (the text binding). Knockout contains many other data-binding types that will be explored throughout the rest of this book.

CHAPTER 4

Working with a Database

There are many options when it comes to working with a database. You can choose anything from SQL Server, Oracle, MySQL, or even a Microsoft Access database! My personal preference is SQL Server. I don't claim it to be the best; however, I do think it is the best choice when working with MVC. ASP.NET and the MVC framework are built and maintained by Microsoft. Microsoft is also the owner of SQL Server. Because of this, I think it provides the best support.

Just like databases, there are a variety of ways to integrate a database into your MVC application. You can write your own SQL statements and access the database by using the classes under the SqlClient (*http://bit.ly/sql-client*) namespace. Or you can use an ORM (Object-Relational-Mapper) that wraps your database access.

What Is an ORM?

An ORM converts a database table into a model, which allows you to use it like any other class in a project. For example, in Chapter 3, a `Person` class was created. With an ORM, this class could be mapped to a Person table.

When you fetch the object from your database, the ORM would return the `Person` class populated with the data. Likewise, saving data to the database would involve creating a new `Person` object populated with the data to save.

My preference is the latter. A framework like Entity Framework (EF) makes it easy to create, access, and maintain your database with an MVC project.

There are several other frameworks like EF, such as NHibernate; however, like SQL Server, Entity Framework is built and maintained by Microsoft, which will provide better support within your application for compatibility.

Chapter 5 will demonstrate this with Visual Studio's built-in support for Entity Framework when creating controllers and views.

Introduction to Entity Framework

Entity Framework is an ORM that provides easy access to your database using LINQ that is written similarly to SQL. EF converts the LINQ to SQL and executes against your database. When the SQL is executed, EF takes the response of your query and converts the results into your models for easy access within your code.

Entity Framework provides three different workflows that you can set up and use within your project:

Database First
> This flow is for when you have an existing database or want complete control over how your database is created and maintained. When you use this flow, you create an EDMX file that stores your data schema, data models, and the relationship between your schema and models in XML. Visual Studio provides a very nice designer that visually displays your model and relationships within it.

Model First
> This flow is quite similar to Database First in that your models and relationships are maintained within an EDMX file. Instead of the EDMX being generated automatically from a database design, you manually create models and define inter-model relationships using the Visual Studio designer. Once finished, you tell EF to create the necessary database tables, columns, and primary and foreign keys. Just like in Database First, the EDMX stores the information in XML.

Code First
> With Code First, you can have Entity Framework automatically create your database. Or if you have an existing database, you can use the Entity Framework tools to create your initial Code First classes. When using Code First, Entity Framework provides a nice toolset that allows you to perform Code First Migrations to automatically update your database when your models change.

The power of the Code First Migrations makes this option extremely convenient for any developer who doesn't require complete control over how the database tables are created and maintained.

Database First makes it very convenient for the opposite scenario—when you want complete control over all database changes, but still want to leverage the power of an ORM.

The next two sections will explore both of these workflows, which will allow you to make your own decision for your projects.

Installing Entity Framework is quite similar to how Knockout was installed using the NuGet Package Manager. To install EF, right-click your project in Visual Studio and select Manage NuGet Packages. Once selected, the NuGet Package Manager will be opened. If it is not already selected, choose the Online option from the left-hand side. Because Entity Framework is so popular, it is often the first result returned. If it is not, type "Entity Framework" in the search box on the right. Once you find it, click the Install button. You will need to accept the licenses agreement before it will be installed in your application.

To demonstrate the differences between Code First and Database First, the next two sections will build a data model that contains a Book model and a related Author model. In this relationship, a Book can have one Author, while an Author can have many Books.

It's time to put the M in MVC! Whether you choose Code First or Database First, interacting with your models will be the same. This will be demonstrated in the next chapter. The remainder of this chapter will focus on creating your models.

Code First

When you use Code First and you don't have an existing database, you need to manually create your Model classes. As mentioned, the example model consists of books and authors. To begin, create a new file called *Book.cs* inside of the *Models* directory. A model is simply a new class with one property per column in your table. Example 4-1 contains the Book model.

Example 4-1. The Book model

```
using System;
using System.Collections.Generic;
using System.Linq;
using System.Web;

namespace BootstrapIntroduction.Models
{
  public class Book
  {
    public int Id { get; set; }

    public int AuthorId { get; set; }

    public string Title { get; set; }

    public string Isbn { get; set; }

    public string Synopsis { get; set; }
```

```
    public string Description { get; set; }

    public string ImageUrl { get; set; }

    public virtual Author Author { get; set; }
  }
}
```

If you try to build your project, it will error out because the Book model contains a reference to the Author model (shown in Example 4-2). Before this code will compile, you must create the Author model, so create a new file called *Author.cs* and add it to the *Models* directory.

Example 4-2. The Author model

```
using System;
using System.Collections.Generic;
using System.Linq;
using System.Web;

namespace BootstrapIntroduction.Models
{
  public class Author
  {
    public int Id { get; set; }

    public string FirstName { get; set; }

    public string LastName { get; set; }

    public string Biography { get; set; }

    public virtual ICollection<Book> Books { get; set; }
  }
}
```

In our data model, a Book can contain one Author. You define this in the Book model by creating the property AuthorId. You also create a virtual property to the Author model, which provides the ability to access the Author model directly from the Book model. Unlike the Book model, the Author model can contain one or more books. Thus, it is defined as a collection of the Book model. When an Author model is accessed, the virtual collection of books provides the ability to display the list of books for a specific author.

Virtual Properties and Lazy Loading

It's quite common to define navigational properties in a model to be virtual. When a navigation property is defined as virtual, it can take advantage of certain Entity Framework functionality. The most common one is lazy loading.

Lazy loading is a nice feature of many ORMs because it allows you to dynamically access related data from a model. It will not unnecessarily fetch the related data until it is actually accessed, thus reducing the up-front querying of data from the database.

Once the models are created, it's time to create a class that maintains your Entity Framework Database Context. The EF context is a lot like a controller in the MVC pattern because it coordinates your data models to the database. It is quite common for a controller to create the `DbContext`. The controller would use your `DbContext` class to fetch the model and pass it to the view.

It's quite common for large projects to have more than one EF context class because you can logically group your models together in one or more contexts. To aid with code organization, it's a good idea to create a new folder in which to store your EF contexts. A common folder name is *DAL*, which stands for Data Access Layer.

With the *DAL* folder created, you can create a new file called *BookContext.cs* inside of it. The `BookContext` (as shown in Example 4-3) contains one `DbSet` property per model in the context. Quite commonly, a `DbSet` is related to a table in the database, and the model represents one row in the table.

Example 4-3. The BookContext

```
using BootstrapIntroduction.Models;
using System;
using System.Collections.Generic;
using System.Data.Entity;
using System.Data.Entity.ModelConfiguration.Conventions;
using System.Linq;
using System.Web;

namespace BootstrapIntroduction.DAL
{
  public class BookContext : DbContext
  {
    public BookContext() : base("BookContext")
    {

    }

    public DbSet<Book> Books { get; set; }
```

```
  public DbSet<Author> Authors { get; set; }

  protected override void OnModelCreating(DbModelBuilder modelBuilder)
  {
    modelBuilder.Conventions.Remove<PluralizingTableNameConvention>();

    base.OnModelCreating(modelBuilder);
  }
 }
}
```

The BookContext is a class that extends the DbContext (*http://msdn.microsoft.com/ en-us/library/system.data.entity.dbcontext(v=VS.103).aspx*) class from Entity Framework. The DbContext class is what allows querying the database. The BookContext class contains an empty constructor that calls the base constructor with the string "BookContext". The DbContext class will use this string to get the connection string from the *Web.config* file so that it can connect to your database.

In this class, I've also added a function that overrides the default OnModelCreat ing function. By overriding this function, I can specify different options for how I want my tables and columns created inside my database. In Example 4-3, I've told EF to remove the convention to pluralize my table names.

Conventions

Entity Framework has a lot of built-in conventions to make database creation easy when using Code First. For example, fields named Id are automatically recognized as primary keys. Likewise, fields with a related class and Id are created as foreign keys. Example 4-1 contains an example of this with the AuthorId property. When EF creates the Book table, it will automatically create a foreign key from AuthorId to the Id of the Author table.

Any of these conventions can be overridden, as demonstrated in Example 4-3, by removing the default to pluralize table names.

Example 4-4 contains an example connection string named BookContext that can be added to the *Web.config* file located in the root of the project. This connection string will use a SQL Server Express LocalDB Database. LocalDB is a lightweight version of SQL Server Express that stores your data inside of MDF files contained within the *App_Data* folder of your project. This is a convenient option for development purposes because it is installed by default with Visual Studio.

Example 4-4. BookContext connection string

```
<connectionStrings>
<add name="BookContext" connectionString=
```

```
    "Data Source=(LocalDb)\v11.0;
     Initial Catalog=BootstrapIntroduction;
     Integrated Security=SSPI;"
     providerName="System.Data.SqlClient"/>
  </connectionStrings>
```

The connection string can be placed anywhere within your *Web.config* file inside of the configuration XML tags. I commonly place mine right below the configSections and above the appSettings section.

Using a Different Database?

If you want to use a different database than the LocalDb, you will need to update the connection string appropriately. You can find more information on Entity Framework Connection Strings (*http://bit.ly/conn-string*) on MSDN.

The models and EF context have now been successfully configured. The next chapter will demonstrate how to add, edit, delete, and fetch data from it.

Database First

For Database First, instead of creating classes to generate the database, you must create the database manually, or you can use an existing database if you have one. Just like in Code First, you can use a LocalDb database for Database First as well.

Let's begin by creating a new LocalDb database. With Visual Studio open, follow these steps:

1. Click View → Server Explorer (Ctrl-Alt-S).
2. Right-click Data Connections and select Add Connection.
3. For the Data Source, select Microsoft SQL Server. There is a checkbox that will let you always use this selection in the future to speed up the process. Click Continue to proceed.
4. The Add Connection dialog will be displayed. See Figure 4-1 for the options I used.

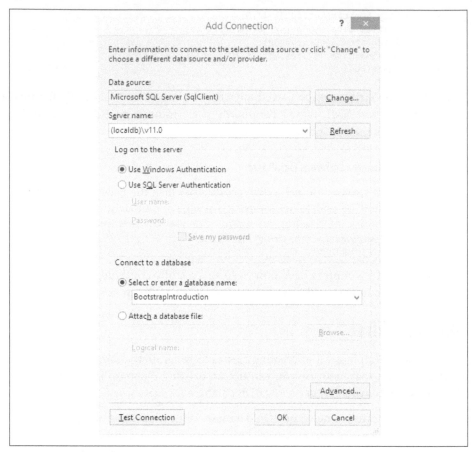

Figure 4-1. The Add Connection dialog box

5. If the database you chose does not exist, you will be prompted to create it. Select Yes to continue.

   The newly created database will now appear under the Data Connections.

With the database created, you can now create tables. Example 4-5 and Example 4-6 contain the SQL to create the Author and Book tables, respectively. To execute the SQL against the database, right-click the BootstrapIntroduction database and select New Query.

Example 4-5. Author table

```
CREATE TABLE [dbo].[Author] (
  [Id] INT IDENTITY (1, 1) NOT NULL,
  [FirstName] NVARCHAR (200) NULL,
  [LastName]  NVARCHAR (200) NULL,
```

```
    [Biography]  NVARCHAR (2000) NULL,
    CONSTRAINT [PK_Author] PRIMARY KEY CLUSTERED ([Id] ASC)
);
```

Click the green play button or press Ctrl-Shift-E to execute the SQL script.

Example 4-6. Book table

```
CREATE TABLE [dbo].[Book] (
    [Id] INT IDENTITY (1, 1) NOT NULL,
    [AuthorId] INT NOT NULL,
    [Title] NVARCHAR (200) NULL,
    [Isbn] NVARCHAR (200) NULL,
    [Synopsis] NVARCHAR (200) NULL,
    [Description] NVARCHAR (2000) NULL,
    [ImageUrl] NVARCHAR (200) NULL,
    CONSTRAINT [PK_Book] PRIMARY KEY CLUSTERED ([Id] ASC),
    CONSTRAINT [FK_Book_Author] FOREIGN KEY ([AuthorId])
        REFERENCES [dbo].[Author] ([Id]) ON DELETE CASCADE
);
```

I've created the same columns in both the Author and Book tables as the Code First example. Example 4-6 also specifies a foreign key from the Book table to the Author table. This will allow Entity Framework to create the proper navigational properties in the next steps.

Once the tables are created, it's time to create the EDMX file that will reverse-engineer the models from the database. Because the end result of the EDMX will create a DbContext (similar to Example 4-3), it should be created inside the previously created *DAL* (Data Access Layer) folder. Follow these steps to create the EDMX:

1. Right-click the *DAL* folder and select Add → New Item.
2. From the left menu, select Data, and if it's not already selected, choose ADO.NET Entity Data Model.
3. For the name, enter "BookDatabaseFirstContext" and click Add. You will now proceed through a wizard to complete the EDMX creation.
4. This will be a Database First EDMX, so select EF Designer from the database and click Next.
5. Now you need to choose the database connection. You'll want to select BookContext (Settings) because this contains the previously created tables. Click Next to continue.
6. In the final step, the database will be read, and a list of objects will be returned. Expand the Tables → dbo menu and select the Author and Book tables. Click Finish to complete the EDMX creation.

After Visual Studio has completed creating and adding the file, the new EDMX will open and should look similar to Figure 4-2.

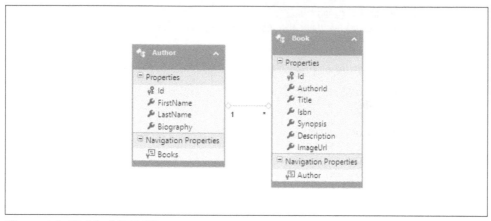

Figure 4-2. Finished EDMX

In the Solution Explorer, if you expand the grouped files under the EDMX, you will see several files with the extension *tt*, which stands for Text Template. These files contain code that will automatically generate your models and `DbContext` from the EDMX file as shown in Figure 4-3.

Figure 4-3. Expanded EDMX

Underneath the *BookDatabaseFirstContext.tt* file are the two models (Author and Book), and underneath the *BookDatabaseFirstContext.Context.tt* file is the `DbContext`. These three files are all autogenerated.

As you can see in Example 4-7, the *BookDatabaseFirstContext.Context.cs* file is almost identical to the `DbContext` created in Example 4-3 with the exception of class names and connection string references.

Example 4-7. Autogenerated DbContext

```
//------------------------------------------------------------------------------
// <auto-generated>
//    This code was generated from a template.
//
```

```
//     Manual changes to this file may cause unexpected behavior in your application.
//     Manual changes to this file will be overwritten if the code is regenerated.
// </auto-generated>
//------------------------------------------------------------------------------

namespace BootstrapIntroduction.DAL
{
    using System;
    using System.Data.Entity;
    using System.Data.Entity.Infrastructure;

    public partial class BootstrapIntroductionEntities : DbContext
    {
        public BootstrapIntroductionEntities()
            : base("name=BootstrapIntroductionEntities")
        {
        }

        protected override void OnModelCreating(DbModelBuilder modelBuilder)
        {
            throw new UnintentionalCodeFirstException();
        }

        public virtual DbSet<Author> Authors { get; set; }
        public virtual DbSet<Book> Books { get; set; }
    }
}
```

The models and `DBContext` have now been automatically generated and whether you choose to continue with Code First or Database First, the next chapter will demonstrate how to add, edit, delete, and fetch data from it.

Creating Test Data

When Entity Framework first accesses a `DbContext`, if the database does not exist, the default behavior will be to create the database and tables. Immediately after this initial creation, EF allows you to provide a class that will automatically seed your database with real or test data.

This example will leverage the `DbContext` from the Code First examples because this database and its tables do not exist yet. Example 4-8 will seed the initial books and authors with books I've previously written. This should be placed in a new file called *BookInitializer.cs* inside the *DAL* folder.

Example 4-8. BookInitializer

```
using BootstrapIntroduction.Models;
using System;
using System.Collections.Generic;
```

```
using System.Data.Entity;
using System.Linq;
using System.Web;

namespace BootstrapIntroduction.DAL
{
  public class BookInitializer : DropCreateDatabaseIfModelChanges<BookContext>
  {
  protected override void Seed(BookContext context)
  {
    var author = new Author
    {
      Biography = "...",
      FirstName = "Jamie",
      LastName = "Munro"
    };

    var books = new List<Book>
    {
      new Book {
      Author = author,
      Description = "...",
      ImageUrl = "http://ecx.images-amazon.com/images/I/51T%2BWt430bL._AA160_.jpg",
      Isbn = "1491914319",
      Synopsis = "...",
      Title = "Knockout.js: Building Dynamic Client-Side Web Applications"
      },
      new Book {
      Author = author,
      Description = "...",
      ImageUrl = "http://ecx.images-amazon.com/images/I/51AkFkNeUxL._AA160_.jpg",
      Isbn = "1449319548",
      Synopsis = "...",
      Title = "20 Recipes for Programming PhoneGap: Cross-Platform Mobile Development"
      },
      new Book {
      Author = author,
      Description = "...",
      ImageUrl = "http://ecx.images-amazon.com/images/I/51LpqnDq8-L._AA160_.jpg",
      Isbn = "1449309860",
      Synopsis = "...",
      Title = "20 Recipes for Programming MVC 3: Faster, Smarter Web Development"
      },
      new Book {
      Author = author,
      Description = "...",
      ImageUrl = "http://ecx.images-amazon.com/images/I/41JC54HEroL._AA160_.jpg",
      Isbn = "1460954394",
      Synopsis = "...",
      Title = "Rapid Application Development With CakePHP"
       }
    };
```

```
        books.ForEach(b => context.Books.Add(b));

        context.SaveChanges();
    }
  }
}
```

To seed the data, you simply create new objects of the model classes. Example 4-8 creates a single Author and a collection of Books. To save the data, you add each book to the Books `DbSet` in the `BookContext`. Finally, you call the `SaveChanges` function on the `BookContext`. When `SaveChanges` is called, EF will commit the changes to the database in a single transaction.

Saving the Author

If you notice in Example 4-8, the Author was not added to the Authors `DbSet`. This is the magic of EF, and it automatically knows that it needs to create the Author prior to saving the book because the Book model was initialized with a reference to the Author.

Configuration is required to complete the initialization process (shown in Example 4-9). Inside the *global.asax.cs* file, the `Application_Start` function will be updated to instantiate the `BookContext`, the `BookInitializer`, and tell the `DbContext` to initialize the database.

Example 4-9. Application_Start

```
using BootstrapIntroduction.DAL;
using System;
using System.Collections.Generic;
using System.Data.Entity;
using System.Linq;
using System.Web;
using System.Web.Mvc;
using System.Web.Optimization;
using System.Web.Routing;

namespace BootstrapIntroduction
{
  public class MvcApplication : System.Web.HttpApplication
  {
    protected void Application_Start()
    {
      AreaRegistration.RegisterAllAreas();
      FilterConfig.RegisterGlobalFilters(GlobalFilters.Filters);
      RouteConfig.RegisterRoutes(RouteTable.Routes);
      BundleConfig.RegisterBundles(BundleTable.Bundles);
```

```
        var bookContext = new BookContext();
        Database.SetInitializer(new BookInitializer());
        bookContext.Database.Initialize(true);
      }
    }
}
```

When the application runs for the first time, it will execute the database initialization and create the one author and four books.

Database Initializers

In Example 4-8, the `BookInitializer` extended the class `DropCrea teDatabaseIfModelChanges`. This tells EF that when it detects a change in the database, it should drop the database and recreate it, and then seed it with the provided data.

There are two other options as well: `CreateDatabaseIfNotExists` and `DropCreateDatabaseAlways`. The first one is the default and is quite common for production because you don't want to be dropping the database each time it changes.

Summary

Although I suggest using SQL Server and Entity Framework for the database and ORM, you are certainly not limited to them. The support that both Visual Studio and Microsoft provides for them, though, make it worthwhile because there are many benefits when using them.

The next chapter will explore scaffolding of controllers and views, and a prerequisite to this is having Entity Framework and a database initialized like this chapter has done.

Going forward, I will be using Code First with Entity Framework because I find it translates better in examples for this book. Database First also works great; in fact, I use it on a day-to-day basis at work because my company wants complete control over all aspects of the database.

PART II

Working with Data

PART III

Working with Data

Listing, Sorting, and Paging Through Tables

It's time to fully integrate MVC, Bootstrap, and Knockout.js together in one example. This will be done by creating a new controller, views, and data binding with Knockout using the data that was prepopulated in Chapter 4. To aid in stubbing out the controllers and views, I am going to use Visual Studio's scaffolding functionality.

Scaffolding is why I choose MVC and Entity Framework in my projects. When I use scaffolding, I find that I can rapidly create websites that provide basic CRUD (Create-Read-Update-Delete) functionality on any model.

This chapter will extend on the Code First `DbContext` and models created in Chapter 4.

Scaffolding the Author Model

Scaffolding involves creating a new controller. To do this, right-click the *Controllers* folder and select Add → Controller. This will start a wizard to create the new controller. In the first step, select MVC 5 Controller with views, using Entity Framework, and click Add to continue.

The Add Controller window will now be displayed (shown in Figure 5-1). It requires three pieces of configuration to complete the scaffolding process:

- For the model class, select Author (BootstrapIntroduction.Models).
- For the data context class, select BookContext (BootstrapIntroduction.DAL). When you selected the model, the controller name field was automatically populated with AuthorsController. Leaving as-is is perfect.
- The Use a layout page option is left checked and empty because the default layout will be used unless otherwise specified. Because there is only one default layout in this project, you don't need to change it.

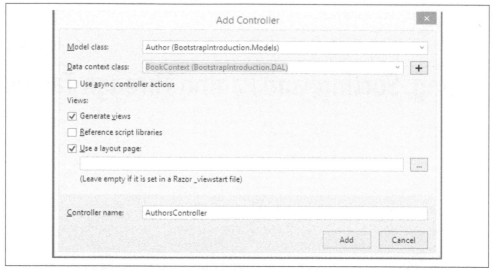

Figure 5-1. Creating the AuthorsController

Click Add to finish creating the `AuthorsController` and its related views. Visual Studio will now scaffold the controller and the views for the new controller.

Error Creating Controller?

During my first attempt, I received an error creating the controller because I had the same models twice; once in the Code First and once in the Database First. Because I no longer require the EDMX from the Database First example, I have deleted this file and its child files.

Along with the `AuthorsController`, Visual Studio also created a new folder called *Authors* under the *Views* directory. Inside this directory are five different views. Each view is used for a different piece of the CRUD process (with the exception of Index and Details because they both are used in the "R").

Example 5-1 contains the scaffolded `AuthorsController` that Visual Studio created.

Example 5-1. The AuthorsController

```
using System;
using System.Collections.Generic;
using System.Data;
using System.Data.Entity;
using System.Linq;
using System.Net;
using System.Web;
```

```
using System.Web.Mvc;
using BootstrapIntroduction.DAL;
using BootstrapIntroduction.Models;

namespace BootstrapIntroduction.Controllers
{
  public class AuthorsController : Controller
  {
    private BookContext db = new BookContext();

    // GET: Authors
    public ActionResult Index()
    {
      return View(db.Authors.ToList());
    }

    // GET: Authors/Details/5
    public ActionResult Details(int? id)
    {
      if (id == null)
      {
        return new HttpStatusCodeResult(HttpStatusCode.BadRequest);
      }
      Author author = db.Authors.Find(id);
      if (author == null)
      {
        return HttpNotFound();
      }
      return View(author);
    }

    // GET: Authors/Create
    public ActionResult Create()
    {
      return View();
    }

    // POST: Authors/Create
    [HttpPost]
    [ValidateAntiForgeryToken]
    public ActionResult Create(
        [Bind(Include = "Id,FirstName,LastName,Biography")] Author author)
    {
      if (ModelState.IsValid)
      {
        db.Authors.Add(author);
        db.SaveChanges();
        return RedirectToAction("Index");
      }

      return View(author);
    }
```

```csharp
// GET: Authors/Edit/5
public ActionResult Edit(int? id)
{
  if (id == null)
  {
    return new HttpStatusCodeResult(HttpStatusCode.BadRequest);
  }
  Author author = db.Authors.Find(id);
  if (author == null)
  {
    return HttpNotFound();
  }
  return View(author);
}

// POST: Authors/Edit/5
[HttpPost]
[ValidateAntiForgeryToken]
public ActionResult Edit(
      [Bind(Include = "Id,FirstName,LastName,Biography")] Author author)
{
  if (ModelState.IsValid)
  {
    db.Entry(author).State = EntityState.Modified;
    db.SaveChanges();
    return RedirectToAction("Index");
  }
  return View(author);
}

// GET: Authors/Delete/5
public ActionResult Delete(int? id)
{
  if (id == null)
  {
    return new HttpStatusCodeResult(HttpStatusCode.BadRequest);
  }
  Author author = db.Authors.Find(id);
  if (author == null)
  {
    return HttpNotFound();
  }
  return View(author);
}

// POST: Authors/Delete/5
[HttpPost, ActionName("Delete")]
[ValidateAntiForgeryToken]
public ActionResult DeleteConfirmed(int id)
{
  Author author = db.Authors.Find(id);
```

```
        db.Authors.Remove(author);
        db.SaveChanges();
        return RedirectToAction("Index");
    }

    protected override void Dispose(bool disposing)
    {
        if (disposing)
        {
            db.Dispose();
        }
        base.Dispose(disposing);
    }
  }
}
```

The AuthorsController, just like the HomeController extends the Controller class. However, unlike the HomeController, each method is not quite so empty. Visual Studio has created all of the necessary methods and functionality to perform CRUD on the authors.

This chapter will focus strictly on the Index function which—using the BookContext —fetches the complete list of authors. The results of this are then passed to the *Index.cshtml* view.

A private variable called db is instantiated as a new BookContext. This will happen at the start of each request from the web browser. The BookContext opens a connection to the database, so it is important that at the end of the request, the BookContext is disposed of properly, closing all open connections to prevent memory leaks. This is done by overriding the Dispose function from the base Controller class. Inside the function, the db variable is disposed. The Dispose function is called by MVC at the end of each request.

Fetching the list of authors is done by accessing the Authors DbSet from the BookContext and calling ToList.

ToList

The access to the Authors `DbSet` is followed by a call to the `ToList` function. This is an important concept when working with Entity Framework. When you are interacting with a `DbSet`, EF doesn't execute any database queries until the data is actually accessed in code. By calling `ToList`, this tells EF to execute the query and populate the list of authors in a list.

Prior to specifying the `ToList` function, you can add filters to the `DbSet` to limit the results. Each time you do this, EF updates the query that will be sent to the database server. Once the data has been queried from the database, any further manipulations to the results will be done strictly on the in-memory object and not against the database.

So far, the M and C have been implemented. Let's complete this example by implementing the V and the VM. The default `Index` view that was created by Visual Studio uses a Razor `foreach` function to show the data. Example 5-2 will change this and implement similar functionality by using the Knockout `foreach` binding to create the table of author data.

Example 5-2. HTML to create table

```
@model IEnumerable<BootstrapIntroduction.Models.Author>
@{
  ViewBag.Title = "Authors";
}

<h2>Authors</h2>

<p>@Html.ActionLink("Create New", "Create")</p>

<table class="table table-bordered table-striped">
  <thead>
    <tr>
      <th>@Html.DisplayNameFor(model => model.FirstName)</th>
      <th>@Html.DisplayNameFor(model => model.LastName)</th>
      <th>Actions</th>
    </tr>
  </thead>
  <tbody data-bind="foreach: authors">
    <tr>
      <td data-bind="text: FirstName"></td>
      <td data-bind="text: LastName"></td>
      <td>
        <a data-bind="attr: { href: '@Url.Action("Details")/' + Id }"
                   class="btn btn-info">Details</a>
        <a data-bind="attr: { href: '@Url.Action("Edit")/' + Id }"
```

```
                    class="btn btn-primary">Edit</a>
        <a data-bind="attr: { href: '@Url.Action("Delete")/' + Id }"
                    class="btn btn-danger">Delete</a>
        </td>
      </tr>
    </tbody>
</table>
```

The view starts with the model binding. In this example, it is an IEnumerable of the
Author model. The next important piece is the definition of the table of data. Instead
of using a Razor foreach loop to display each author, inside the tbody tag there is an
HTML attribute called data-bind that is defined as foreach: authors. When the
Knockout bindings are applied, the block of HTML code contained within the tbody
will be repeated for each element in the list.

Inside the tbody is a td tag for each column in the table. The td tag is using the text
data binding for each column. And finally, three buttons are created allowing you to
navigate to the details, edit, and delete of that author. Each button is using another
new data binding called attr. This binding lets you create any HTML attribute. In
this example, it is setting the href attribute for each link. This is a great example of
mixing Razor with Knockout. The UrlHelper is used to generate the link to *Authors/
Edit* and then the author ID is appended to the end of the link from the Knockout
binding.

More code is required to complete this example. Example 5-3 should be added to the
Authors/Index view after the end of the table.

Example 5-3. The ViewModel

```
@section Scripts {
  <script>
    function ViewModel(authors) {
      var self = this;

      self.authors = authors;
    };

    var viewModel = new ViewModel(@Html.HtmlConvertToJson(Model));
    ko.applyBindings(viewModel);
  </script>
}
```

This example creates a new ViewModel that accepts an array of authors in its constructor. This array is then assigned to a local property also called authors. This
property is what the view was data bound to in the foreach binding.

The ViewModel is then instantiated with the model that was provided from the controller. The model is converted into a JavaScript array by calling a custom `HtmlHelper` extension (shown in Example 5-4).

Example 5-4. HtmlHelper extension

```
using Newtonsoft.Json;
using System.Web;
using System.Web.Mvc;

public static class HtmlHelperExtensions
{
  public static HtmlString HtmlConvertToJson(this HtmlHelper htmlHelper,
object model)
  {
    var settings = new JsonSerializerSettings
    {
      ReferenceLoopHandling = ReferenceLoopHandling.Ignore,
      Formatting = Formatting.Indented
    };

    return new HtmlString(JsonConvert.SerializeObject(model, settings));
  }
}
```

This example should be placed inside a new file called *HtmlHelperExtension* inside a new folder called *Extensions*. This extension method accepts a model object and uses a third-party library to serialize the data into a JavaScript object. The third-party library is called Json.Net and should be installed via the NuGet Package Manager. To install the package, follow these steps:

1. Right-click the Project and select Manage NuGet Packages.
2. If it is not already selected, on the left, choose Online.
3. Select Json.Net. (This is an extremely popular package, and is typically second in the list.)
4. Click the Install button to add this to your project.

Running the completed example will show results similar to Figure 5-2.

Figure 5-2. The list of authors

Sorting the Authors

The default functionality after scaffolding the authors is quite nice, but there are defi-nitely some missing pieces, such as sorting and paging through the results. This sec-tion will update the controller and view to provide the ability to sort the authors.

Sorting data involves manipulating the `DbSet` with LINQ statements. For example, to return the list of authors sorted by first name, you would use `db.Authors.OrderBy(a => a.FirstName).ToList()`.

When using LINQ, it is strongly typed to your model. Many tutorials would then demonstrate sorting your data by creating a `switch` statement for each field in your model that should be sorted. I find this tedious to maintain and not extremely flexible.

Once again, there is a great third-party library that provides support for dynamic LINQ statements. With a dynamic LINQ statement, a string can be used to define the field to be sorted on. For example, the string `"FirstName ASC"` would result to the same `db.Authors.OrderBy(a => a.FirstName)`. These next few examples will demonstrate it.

To begin, the new library needs to be installed via NuGet. Open the NuGet Package Manager and search for "dynamic." The first result should be System.Linq.Dynamic. Click Install to add it to your project.

Example 5-5 creates a new model called `QueryOptions`. This class will store the sort-ing and paging options. For now, this class will contain only the fields for sorting.

Example 5-5. QueryOptions model

```
namespace BootstrapIntroduction.Models
{
  public class QueryOptions
  {
    public QueryOptions()
    {
      SortField = "Id";
      SortOrder = SortOrder.ASC;
    }

    public string SortField { get; set; }

    public SortOrder SortOrder { get; set; }

    public string Sort
    {
      get
      {
        return string.Format("{0} {1}",
          SortField, SortOrder.ToString());
      }
    }
  }
}
```

The QueryOptions class contains two properties that can be read and written to: Sort
Field and SortOrder. The SortField defines which field from the model should be
sorted on. The SortOrder field indicates the direction. There is also a third property
that is read-only. This property concatenates the two properties into a single string.
This will be used in the dynamic LINQ. This model will be used in the controller to
order the authors prior to passing to the view.

The QueryOptions model references an enum called SortOrder. This enum is shown
in Example 5-6 and should be added to the *Models* folder. The SortOrder could be
accomplished without the use of an enum; however, then it would involve comparing
strings. An enum allows us to use strongly typed comparisons.

Example 5-6. SortOrder enum

```
namespace BootstrapIntroduction.Models
{
  public enum SortOrder
  {
    ASC,
    DESC
  }
}
```

Now the `Index` in the `AuthorsController` (shown in Example 5-7) can be updated to accept the `QueryOptions` class as input. This class is then used to order the authors by leveraging the dynamic LINQ library that was previously added.

Example 5-7. AuthorsController

```
using System;
using System.Collections.Generic;
using System.Data;
using System.Data.Entity;
using System.Linq;
using System.Linq.Dynamic;
using System.Net;
using System.Web;
using System.Web.Mvc;
using BootstrapIntroduction.DAL;
using BootstrapIntroduction.Models;
using System.Web.ModelBinding;

namespace BootstrapIntroduction.Controllers
{
  public class AuthorsController : Controller
  {
    private BookContext db = new BookContext();

    // GET: Authors
    public ActionResult Index([Form] QueryOptions queryOptions)
    {
      var authors = db.Authors.OrderBy(queryOptions.Sort);

      ViewBag.QueryOptions = queryOptions;

      return View(authors.ToList());
    }

    // other functions removed for an abbreviated example
  }
}
```

As you'll see in Example 5-8, the view will build a URL that contains the `SortField` and `SortOrder`. By adding the `[Form]` attribute in front of the `QueryOptions` parameter, MVC will automatically parse the URL parameters and create the `QueryOptions` class for us. If the URL contains no fields, it will simply create a new `QueryOptions` class without setting the `SortField` and `SortOrder` properties. In Example 5-5, these are instantiated in the constructor to be "Id" and ascending.

The `QueryOptions` are passed to the view by using the `ViewBag` property. The view will use this to help build the URL by inversing the sort direction for the current field being sorted.

Example 5-8 contains an updated Index view.

Example 5-8. Authors Index view

```
@using BootstrapIntroduction.Models
@model IEnumerable<Author>

@{
  ViewBag.Title = "Authors";
  var queryOptions = (QueryOptions)ViewBag.QueryOptions;
}

<h2>Authors</h2>

<p>@Html.ActionLink("Create New", "Create")</p>

<table class="table table-bordered table-striped">
  <thead>
    <tr>
      <th>@Html.BuildSortableLink("First Name", "Index", "FirstName"
        , queryOptions)</th>
      <th>@Html.BuildSortableLink("Last Name", "Index", "LastName"
        , queryOptions)</th>
      <th>Actions</th>
    </tr>
  </thead>
  <tbody data-bind="foreach: authors">
    <tr>
      <td data-bind="text: FirstName"></td>
      <td data-bind="text: LastName"></td>
      <td>
        <a data-bind="attr: { href: '@Url.Action("Details")/' + Id }"
                 class="btn btn-info">Details</a>
        <a data-bind="attr: { href: '@Url.Action("Edit")/' + Id }"
                 class="btn btn-primary">Edit</a>
        <a data-bind="attr: { href: '@Url.Action("Delete")/' + Id }"
                 class="btn btn-danger">Delete</a>
      </td>
    </tr>
  </tbody>
</table>

@section Scripts {
  <script>
    function ViewModel(authors) {
      var self = this;

      self.authors = authors;
    };

    var viewModel = new ViewModel(@Html.HtmlConvertToJson(Model));
    ko.applyBindings(viewModel);
```

```
      </script>
}
```

The `QueryOptions` that was passed from the controller in the `ViewBag` property is cas-
ted from the dynamic property and stored in a local variable that the view can access.
The other major change converts the static text in the `th` tag to build a link back to
the index page with the URL parameters defining the sort direction.

The link is built using another custom `HtmlHelper` extension. Example 5-9 contains
an updated `HtmlHelperExtension` that creates a new function called `BuildSortable
Link` that accepts four parameters:

fieldName
> This is the name of the link (e.g., First Name).

actionName
> This is the name of the action to link to (e.g., Index).

sortField
> This is the name of the model field to sort on (e.g., FirstName).

queryOptions
> This contains the `QueryOptions` currently used to sort the authors. This is used
> to determine if the current field is being sorted, in which case the direction
> should be inversed.

This function returns an `MvcHtmlString` with the link that, when selected, will reload
the page and sort the authors by the specified field in the specified order.

Example 5-9. HtmlHelperExtension

```
using BootstrapIntroduction.Models;
using Newtonsoft.Json;
using System.Web;
using System.Web.Mvc;
using System.Web.Mvc.Html;

public static class HtmlHelperExtensions
{
  public static HtmlString HtmlConvertToJson(this HtmlHelper htmlHelper
    , object model)
  {
    var settings = new JsonSerializerSettings
    {
      ReferenceLoopHandling = ReferenceLoopHandling.Ignore,
      Formatting = Formatting.Indented
    };

    return new HtmlString(JsonConvert.SerializeObject(model, settings));
```

```
    }

    public static MvcHtmlString BuildSortableLink(this HtmlHelper htmlHelper,
        string fieldName, string actionName, string sortField, QueryOptions queryOptions)
    {
        var urlHelper = new UrlHelper(htmlHelper.ViewContext.RequestContext);

        var isCurrentSortField = queryOptions.SortField == sortField;

        return new MvcHtmlString(string.Format("<a href=\"{0}\">{1} {2}</a>",
            urlHelper.Action(actionName,
            new {
                SortField = sortField,
                SortOrder = (isCurrentSortField
                    && queryOptions.SortOrder == SortOrder.ASC)
                  ? SortOrder.DESC : SortOrder.ASC
            }),
            fieldName,
            BuildSortIcon(isCurrentSortField, queryOptions)));
    }

    private static string BuildSortIcon(bool isCurrentSortField
        , QueryOptions queryOptions)
    {
        string sortIcon = "sort";

        if (isCurrentSortField)
        {
            sortIcon += "-by-alphabet";
            if (queryOptions.SortOrder == SortOrder.DESC)
                sortIcon += "-alt";
        }

        return string.Format("<span class=\"{0} {1}{2}\"></span>",
            "glyphicon", "glyphicon-", sortIcon);
    }
}
```

As a nice little touch, Example 5-9 contains a private function called `BuildSortIcon`
that leverages three of the many glyphicons provided by Bootstrap. When the field is
not currently being sorted, it uses the `glyphicon-sort`. When the field is being sorted
ascending, it uses the `glyphicon-sort-by-alphabet`. And when the field is being
sorted descending, it uses `glyphicon-sort-by-alphabet-alt`.

Figure 5-3 demonstrates the sorting in action.

Figure 5-3. Authors sorted by last name descending

When you run this example, it will be difficult to see the sorting in action. However, this can be solved by clicking the link to create a new author (as I've shown in Figure 5-3) and use the previously scaffolded view and controller action to create a new author. Once you've created additional authors, you can click the first and last name links to sort them. Clicking the same link twice will alter the direction from ascending to descending, and vice versa.

Paging the Authors

Paging through the authors is quite similar to sorting. LINQ will be used on the `DbSet` to `Skip` and `Take` a specific number of records. The previously created `QueryOp tions` model will be updated (shown in Example 5-10) to include three new properties: `CurrentPage`, `TotalPages`, and `PageSize`. `CurrentPage` and `PageSize` have been defaulted to 1 in the constructor. One is a very small number for the page size; however, when dealing with a small number of authors, it makes it easier to test the functionality. Ten is a more common number for paging.

Example 5-10. Updated QueryOptions model

```
namespace BootstrapIntroduction.Models
{
  public class QueryOptions
  {
    public QueryOptions()
    {
      CurrentPage = 1;
      PageSize = 1;

      SortField = "Id";
      SortOrder = SortOrder.ASC;
    }

    public int CurrentPage { get; set; }

    public int TotalPages { get; set; }

    public int PageSize { get; set; }

    public string SortField { get; set; }

    public SortOrder SortOrder { get; set; }

    public string Sort
    {
      get
      {
        return string.Format("{0} {1}",
          SortField, SortOrder.ToString());
      }
    }
  }
}
```

In Example 5-11, the `AuthorsController` `Index` function has been updated to implement the LINQ to skip and take the specific number of records. Inside this updated function, the `TotalPages` from the `QueryOptions` model (the one that was not defaulted in the constructor) is set by calculating the number of pages from the count of authors divided by the page size, rounded up. This will be used in the view to disable the Next button.

Example 5-11. Updated AuthorsController

```
using System;
using System.Collections.Generic;
using System.Data;
using System.Data.Entity;
using System.Linq;
using System.Linq.Dynamic;
using System.Net;
using System.Web;
using System.Web.Mvc;
using BootstrapIntroduction.DAL;
using BootstrapIntroduction.Models;
using System.Web.ModelBinding;

namespace BootstrapIntroduction.Controllers
{
  public class AuthorsController : Controller
  {
    private BookContext db = new BookContext();

    // GET: Authors
    public ActionResult Index([Form] QueryOptions queryOptions)
    {
      var start = (queryOptions.CurrentPage - 1) * queryOptions.PageSize;

      var authors = db.Authors.
        OrderBy(queryOptions.Sort).
        Skip(start).
        Take(queryOptions.PageSize);

      queryOptions.TotalPages =
        (int)Math.Ceiling((double)db.Authors.Count() / queryOptions.PageSize);

      ViewBag.QueryOptions = queryOptions;

      return View(authors.ToList());
    }

    // other functions removed for an abbreviated example
  }
}
```

Just like when sorting the authors, the logic to generate the HTML for paging the authors has been done inside another custom HtmlHelper method. Example 5-12 creates one public function called BuildNextPreviousLinks that accepts the QueryOptions and the actionName as input parameters. Four private functions are also created to build the necessary HTML to generate the next and previous links shown in Figure 5-4.

Example 5-12. Updated HtmlHelperExtension

```
using BootstrapIntroduction.Models;
using Newtonsoft.Json;
using System.Web;
using System.Web.Mvc;
using System.Web.Mvc.Html;

public static class HtmlHelperExtensions
{
  public static MvcHtmlString BuildNextPreviousLinks(
        this HtmlHelper htmlHelper, QueryOptions queryOptions, string actionName)
  {
    var urlHelper = new UrlHelper(htmlHelper.ViewContext.RequestContext);

    return new MvcHtmlString(string.Format(
"<nav>" +
"    <ul class=\"pager\">" +
"        <li class=\"previous {0}\">{1}</li>" +
"        <li class=\"next {2}\">{3}</li>" +
"    </ul>" +
"</nav>",
    IsPreviousDisabled(queryOptions),
    BuildPreviousLink(urlHelper, queryOptions, actionName),
    IsNextDisabled(queryOptions),
    BuildNextLink(urlHelper, queryOptions, actionName)
    ));
  }

  private static string IsPreviousDisabled(QueryOptions queryOptions)
  {
    return (queryOptions.CurrentPage == 1)
      ? "disabled" : string.Empty;
  }

  private static string IsNextDisabled(QueryOptions queryOptions)
  {
    return (queryOptions.CurrentPage == queryOptions.TotalPages)
      ? "disabled" : string.Empty;
  }

  private static string BuildPreviousLink(
      UrlHelper urlHelper, QueryOptions queryOptions, string actionName)
  {
    return string.Format(
      "<a href=\"{0}\"><span aria-hidden=\"true\">&larr;</span> Previous</a>",
      urlHelper.Action(actionName, new
      {
        SortOrder = queryOptions.SortOrder,
        SortField = queryOptions.SortField,
        CurrentPage = queryOptions.CurrentPage - 1,
        PageSize = queryOptions.PageSize
```

```
        }));
    }

    private static string BuildNextLink(
        UrlHelper urlHelper, QueryOptions queryOptions, string actionName)
    {
      return string.Format(
        "<a href=\"{0}\">Next <span aria-hidden=\"true\">&rarr;</span></a>",
        urlHelper.Action(actionName, new
        {
          SortOrder = queryOptions.SortOrder,
          SortField = queryOptions.SortField,
          CurrentPage = queryOptions.CurrentPage + 1,
          PageSize = queryOptions.PageSize
        }));
    }

    // other functions removed for an abbreviated example
}
```

The generated next and previous links are leveraging more Bootstrap components for pagination. When you are on the first page, the Previous link is disabled. Similarly, when you are on the last page, the Next link is disabled.

Because the `QueryOptions` are passed into the custom `HtmlHelper` function, the next and previous links include the current sorting options into the URL. The sorting links are not updated because when the sorting direction changes, the current page should be reset back to 1.

Figure 5-4. Next/Previous links

To complete this example, the `Index` view of the `AuthorsController` needs to be updated to execute the `BuildNextPreviousLinks` from the `HtmlHelper`. Example

5-13 contains the one-liner that can be added to the Index view below the end `table` tag.

Example 5-13. Create the next/previous links

```
@Html.BuildNextPreviousLinks(queryOptions, "Index")
```

Summary

This chapter focused on a single part of the CRUD operation, but it introduced several new things from MVC, Bootstrap, and Knockout.

In MVC, LINQ was used to sort a collection and limit the number of results returned. The `HtmlHelper` was extended multiple times to create reusable links to sort the data or navigate between pages.

For Bootstrap, several of the table classes were used to provide alternating row colors, borders, etc. The pagination component was also used to create nicely aligned next and previous links, including disabling the link when on the first and last page.

And finally, Knockout introduced a new `foreach` data binding that repeated a block of HTML code for each element in the array.

CHAPTER 6

Working with Forms

If you experimented in the preceding chapter, you will have noticed that the scaffolded `AuthorsController` is fully functional in terms of adding, editing, and deleting records from the Author table. This in itself makes it quite useful; however, this chapter will demonstrate how to integrate Knockout and Bootstrap into the form as well as a little jQuery to submit the form via AJAX.

Upgrading Bootstrap

When I introduced the NuGet Package Manager, I mentioned updating the existing packages to their latest versions. The version that is installed with MVC is version 3.0 and some of the features used in this chapter (and future chapters) use the documentation from version 3.3.

If you didn't update the packages back in Chapter 3, I would encourage you to do it now by following these steps:

1. Right-click the project and select Manage NuGet Packages.
2. On the left, select the Update option. This will search online for any updates to all of the packages currently installed.
3. If you are comfortable with updating all packages, you can click the Update All button, or you can find just the Bootstrap package and update it individually.

Integrating Knockout with a Form

This chapter will start to demonstrate why I love working with these three technologies together. It's going to take a nice-looking form and add some usability to it. In fact, no changes are required to the `AuthorsController`.

Back in Chapter 4 when the Author and Book models were created, I didn't specify any data validation for them. Because jQuery provides good client-side validation that integrates nicely with MVC, I thought I would go back and add some validation on the Author model.

Example 6-1 demonstrates making both the first and last name required fields before saving to the database.

Example 6-1. Updated AuthorModel

```
using System;
using System.Collections.Generic;
using System.ComponentModel.DataAnnotations;
using System.Linq;
using System.Web;

namespace BootstrapIntroduction.Models
{
  public class Author
  {
    public int Id { get; set; }

    [Required]
    public string FirstName { get; set; }

    [Required]
    public string LastName { get; set; }

    public string Biography { get; set; }

    public virtual ICollection<Book> Books { get; set; }
  }
}
```

Above the definition of both the first and last name properties, an attribute has been added called Required. This does several things. In the AuthorsController, the create method performs a ModelState.IsValid check, which validates that all properties of the model are valid based upon all of the validation rules identified. And secondly, as mentioned, jQuery validation will perform client-side validations by taking the rules in the model and implementing them via JavaScript.

More Validation

MVC provides a variety of validation options apart from the afore-mentioned `Required` attribute, such as minimum string length, regular expressions, minimum and maximum integer values, etc. Throughout this book, we will explore several as they are required. A list of attribute classes can be found at MSDN under the DataAnnotations namespace (*http://bit.ly/data-anno*).

With the validation implemented on the `Author` model, it's time to move on to the UI and Knockout data bindings. Example 6-2 contains the Knockout ViewModel called `AuthorFormViewModel`. To allow for easy management of the various ViewModels, I suggest creating a new folder called *ViewModels* inside the *Scripts* folder. Code organization is a very important step in building maintainable code. Right-click the *Scripts* folder and select the Add submenu item followed by New Folder. Once the new folder is created, create a new JavaScript file called *AuthorFormViewModel.js*.

Example 6-2. AuthorFormViewModel

```
function AuthorFormViewModel() {
  var self = this;

  self.saveCompleted = ko.observable(false);
  self.sending = ko.observable(false);

  self.author = {
    firstName: ko.observable(),
    lastName: ko.observable(),
    biography: ko.observable(),
  };

  self.validateAndSave = function (form) {
    if (!$(form).valid())
      return false;

    self.sending(true);

    // include the anti forgery token
    self.author.__RequestVerificationToken = form[0].value;

    $.ajax({
      url: 'Create',
      type: 'post',
      contentType: 'application/x-www-form-urlencoded',
      data: ko.toJS(self.author)
    })
    .success(self.successfulSave)
    .error(self.errorSave)
    .complete(function () { self.sending(false) });
```

```
  };

  self.successfulSave = function () {
    self.saveCompleted(true);

    $('.body-content').prepend(
         '<div class="alert alert-success">
         <strong>Success!</strong> The new author has been saved.</div>');
    setTimeout(function () { location.href = './'; }, 1000);
  };

  self.errorSave = function () {
    $('.body-content').prepend(
         '<div class="alert alert-danger">
         <strong>Error!</strong> There was an error creating the author.</div>');
  };
}
```

This file introduces a new concept with Knockout called *observable variables*. When you define a JavaScript variable as an observable, Knockout will begin tracking changes to the variable. This means that if you data bind the observable in your form, Knockout will update the JavaScript variable in your ViewModel; and vice versa, if you update the property in your ViewModel and it is data bound to an HTML element it will be automatically updated when it changes.

Example 6-2 contains five properties marked as observables. The `saveCompleted` observable will be used to alter the page once the new author has been saved successfully. The `sending` observable will be used to show a progress bar when the author is being saved via AJAX and hide the submit button while it's saving. The final three observables are contained within the author structure that are bound to the author form elements. The `author` property with its observables will be submitted via AJAX to save the author.

After the observable variables are three functions: `validateAndSave`, `successful Save`, and `errorSave`. The first function introduces the `submit` data binding and is called by Knockout when the authors form is submitted.

The `validateAndSave` function is doing three important things:

- Not submitting the form if it doesn't pass the jQuery validation.
- Dynamically adding an antiforgery token from the form to the AJAX request.
- Sending the author object via an AJAX form post.

The final two functions are called from the `validateAndSave` function upon success or failure. If saving the author is successful, a new success alert message is added with jQuery at the top of the form, and after one second, the user is redirected back to the list of authors page. Similarly if an error occurs, an error alert is displayed indicating that the author was not saved.

setTimout

Example 6-2 contains a `setTimout` function, which is contained within the `successfulSave` function. It is used to display a success alert message to the user, and then after one second, redirect back to the list of authors.

The final piece of the puzzle is the *Create.cshtml* view. The complete source is displayed in Example 6-7. The next few examples will display the important pieces of implementing Knockout within the view and the creation of a progress bar with Bootstrap. Figure 6-1 demonstrates what the final form looks like, including error messages, because no first and last names were entered.

Create
Author

FirstName		
	The FirstName field is required.	
LastName		
	The LastName field is required.	
Biography		
	Create	

Back to List

Figure 6-1. Creating author with error handling

The form that was created when the view was first scaffolded has been updated to set a data binding for the submit event. Example 6-3 indicates that when the form is submitted, Knockout should call the `validateAndSave` function.

Example 6-3. Submit data binding

```
@using (Html.BeginForm("Create", "Authors", FormMethod.Post,
    new { data_bind = "submit: validateAndSave" }))
```

All three of the form fields (first name, last name, and biography) have been updated to include a   data-binding attribute of `value` (as shown in Example 6-4). Each is bound to the appropriate observable property inside the `author` variable. When the user types into the form field, Knockout will update the corresponding observable property.

Example 6-4. Value data binding

```
@Html.EditorFor(model => model.FirstName, new { htmlAttributes =
    new { @class = "form-control", data_bind = "value: author.firstName" } })
```

In Example 6-5, the submit button is updated to include the `visible` data binding. When the `sending` observable variable is false, the button is visible. When it is true, the button will be hidden so that the user cannot click it multiple times while the author is being saved via AJAX.

Beneath the submit button is where the progress bar is included with the appropriate Bootstrap classes. The `div` tag used to define the progress bar is also decorated with the `visible` data binding. It is using the opposite of the button, meaning it is only visible when the author is being saved via AJAX and hidden when it is not.

Example 6-5. Submit button and progress bar

```
<div class="form-group">
    <div class="col-md-offset-2 col-md-10" data-bind="visible: !sending()">
        <input type="submit" value="Create" class="btn btn-default" />
    </div>

    <div class="progress" data-bind="visible: sending">
        <div class="progress-bar progress-bar-info progress-bar-striped active"
            role="progressbar" aria-valuenow="100"
            aria-valuemin="0" aria-valuemax="100"
            style="width: 100%">
        <span class="sr-only"></span>
        </div>
    </div>
</div>
```

Accessing Observables

When you create an observable property, Knockout converts the variable into a function to track its changes. This means when you want to access the value to the property, you need to add brackets after its name to execute the function.

In Example 6-5, you might have noticed that the submit button has brackets after `sending` and the progress bar does not. Knockout is intelligent enough that when it is comparing to true, brackets are not required because Knockout will detect if it is an observable and automatically add the brackets. On the other hand, when you are saying not (!) `sending`, you need to access the observable variable's value prior to checking if it is false.

The final change made to the `Create` view is to include the `Scripts` section. Example 6-6 includes two JavaScript files: the jQuery Validation bundle (for the unobtrusive form validation) and the `AuthorFormViewModel` that was shown in Example 6-2. After these files are included, the `AuthorFormViewModel` is instantiated and `ko.applyBindings` is called with it.

Example 6-6. Scripts section

```
@section Scripts {
  @Scripts.Render("~/bundles/jqueryval",
      "/Scripts/ViewModels/AuthorFormViewModel.js")
  <script>
    var viewModel = new AuthorFormViewModel();
    ko.applyBindings(viewModel);
  </script>
}
```

Example 6-7 shows the full *Views/Authors/Create.cshtml* file.

Example 6-7. Authors Create view

```
@model BootstrapIntroduction.Models.Author
@{
  ViewBag.Title = "Create";
}

<div data-bind="visible: !saveCompleted()">

  <h2>Create</h2>

  @using (Html.BeginForm("Create", "Authors", FormMethod.Post,
      new { data_bind = "submit: validateAndSave" }))
  {
    @Html.AntiForgeryToken()
```

```
<div class="form-horizontal">
  <h4>Author</h4>
  <hr />
  @Html.ValidationSummary(true, "", new { @class = "text-danger" })
  <div class="form-group">
    @Html.LabelFor(model => model.FirstName, htmlAttributes:
            new { @class = "control-label col-md-2" })
    <div class="col-md-10">
      @Html.EditorFor(model => model.FirstName, new { htmlAttributes =
                new { @class = "form-control",
                    data_bind = "value: author.firstName" } })
      @Html.ValidationMessageFor(model => model.FirstName, "",
                new { @class = "text-danger" })
    </div>
  </div>

  <div class="form-group">
    @Html.LabelFor(model => model.LastName, htmlAttributes:
            new { @class = "control-label col-md-2" })
    <div class="col-md-10">
      @Html.EditorFor(model => model.LastName, new { htmlAttributes =
                new { @class = "form-control", data_bind = "value:
                    author.lastName" } })
      @Html.ValidationMessageFor(model => model.LastName, "",
                new { @class = "text-danger" })
    </div>
  </div>

  <div class="form-group">
    @Html.LabelFor(model => model.Biography, htmlAttributes:
            new { @class = "control-label col-md-2" })
    <div class="col-md-10">
      @Html.EditorFor(model => model.Biography, new { htmlAttributes =
                new { @class = "form-control", data_bind = "value:
                    author.biography" } })
      @Html.ValidationMessageFor(model => model.Biography, "",
                new { @class = "text-danger" })
    </div>
  </div>

  <div class="form-group">
    <div class="col-md-offset-2 col-md-10" data-bind="visible: !sending()">
      <input type="submit" value="Create" class="btn btn-default" />
    </div>

    <div class="progress" data-bind="visible: sending">
      <div class="progress-bar progress-bar-info progress-bar-striped active"
        role="progressbar" aria-valuenow="100"
        aria-valuemin="0" aria-valuemax="100"
        style="width: 100%">
        <span class="sr-only"></span>
```

```
        </div>
      </div>
    </div>
  </div>
  }
</div>

<div>
  @Html.ActionLink("Back to List", "Index")
</div>

@section Scripts {
  @Scripts.Render("~/bundles/jqueryval",
      "/Scripts/ViewModels/AuthorFormViewModel.js")
  <script>
    var viewModel = new AuthorFormViewModel();
    ko.applyBindings(viewModel);
  </script>
}
```

Sharing the View and ViewModel

It's decision time now. The create author view has been updated and integrated with Knockout and some Bootstrap; however, the edit author view is still using the old way. To be consistent (and consistency in a website is important), the edit view should be updated to match the create.

It would be pretty easy to copy all of the changes from the create form to the edit form, making the subtle adjustments where applicable. I personally try to avoid this whenever possible. I instead like to share the View and ViewModel between the two. Sharing the code makes updates easier to maintain. For example, if a new field were added to the Author model, there is less work because once it is added, both the create and edit forms will have it.

Use Caution

While I strongly recommend sharing the View and ViewModel, there are many times when this is not easy or even possible. If the structure of the two are very different or contain different rules, it makes more sense to maintain separate Views and ViewModels. This would be less complicated than a single View and ViewModel with many conditional statements identifying the differences.

Sharing the View and ViewModel involves updating several different things:

1. The AuthorsController needs updating to load the same view (shown in Example 6-8) for the Create and Edit actions.

2. The `Create` function needs to instantiate a new `Author` model and provide this to the view (also shown in Example 6-8). This will be explained in more detail with the following code examples.

3. The `Create` view will be renamed to `Form` to help better identify that it is not specifically for create or edit.

4. The newly renamed `Form` view will contain several conditional statements to change the wording when an author is being added or edited. It will also serialize the `Author` model bound to the view. This will then be passed into the `Author FormViewModel` to prepopulate the author when it is being edited. This is shown in Example 6-9.

5. The `AuthorFormViewModel` author variable contains a new `id` property to distinguish whether the author is being added or edited. This will also be used to update the jQuery AJAX request to either go to the `Create` or `Edit` action (shown in Example 6-10).

6. The `Author` model is updated (shown in Example 6-11) to leverage a new data annotation called `JsonProperty` that will allow the properties to be camelCased when used in JavaScript, but remain PascalCase in C#.

7. The previous model changes also have an effect on the `Index` view because the previously PascalCase variable references now need to be camelCased as shown in Example 6-12.

There are a total of seven things to do, so let's get started. Example 6-8 contains an abbreviated AuthorsController with the required updates to the `Create` and `Edit` functions.

Example 6-8. Updated AuthorsController

```
using System;
using System.Collections.Generic;
using System.Data;
using System.Data.Entity;
using System.Linq;
using System.Linq.Dynamic;
using System.Net;
using System.Web;
using System.Web.Mvc;
using BootstrapIntroduction.DAL;
using BootstrapIntroduction.Models;
using System.Web.ModelBinding;

namespace BootstrapIntroduction.Controllers
{
  public class AuthorsController : Controller
  {
    private BookContext db = new BookContext();
```

```
// Abbreviated controller

// GET: Authors/Create
public ActionResult Create()
{
  return View("Form", new Author());
}

// GET: Authors/Edit/5
public ActionResult Edit(int? id)
{
  if (id == null)
  {
    return new HttpStatusCodeResult(HttpStatusCode.BadRequest);
  }
  Author author = db.Authors.Find(id);
  if (author == null)
  {
    return HttpNotFound();
  }
  return View("Form", author);
}

// Abbreviated controller
}
```

This example completes the first two items on the list. You will notice that the `return` `View` at the end of each method has been updated to pass two parameters. The first parameter is the name of the view to load, in this case, `Form`. The second parameter is the model that is bound to the view. Previously, the `Create` method did not pass this in, even though it was bound to it. However, it is now instantiated as an empty model, because the model will be serialized and passed as a JavaScript object to the `Author` `FormViewModel`. If the `Create` function did not instantiate it, the model would be null, and the JavaScript ViewModel would be unable to parse out the properties.

The `Edit` view that was automatically scaffolded can be safely deleted. The `Create` view should now be renamed to `Form`. This can be done by selecting the view in Visual Studio and pressing F2.

Example 6-9 contains the full `Form` view. The added/altered lines are highlighted to identify them easily.

Example 6-9. Form view

```
@model BootstrapIntroduction.Models.Author
@{
  var isCreating = Model.Id == 0;
  ViewBag.Title = (isCreating) ? "Create" : "Edit";
}
```

```
<div data-bind="visible: !saveCompleted()">

  <h2>@ViewBag.Title</h2>

  @using (Html.BeginForm("Create", "Authors", FormMethod.Post,
      new { data_bind = "submit: validateAndSave" }))
  {
    @Html.AntiForgeryToken()

    <div class="form-horizontal">
      <h4>Author</h4>
      <hr />
      @Html.ValidationSummary(true, "", new { @class = "text-danger" })
      <div class="form-group">
        @Html.LabelFor(model => model.FirstName, htmlAttributes:
                  new { @class = "control-label col-md-2" })
        <div class="col-md-10">
          @Html.EditorFor(model => model.FirstName, new { htmlAttributes =
                      new { @class = "form-control",
                          data_bind = "value: author.firstName" } })
          @Html.ValidationMessageFor(model => model.FirstName, "",
                      new { @class = "text-danger" })
        </div>
      </div>

      <div class="form-group">
        @Html.LabelFor(model => model.LastName, htmlAttributes:
                  new { @class = "control-label col-md-2" })
        <div class="col-md-10">
          @Html.EditorFor(model => model.LastName, new { htmlAttributes =
                      new { @class = "form-control",
                          data_bind = "value: author.lastName" } })
          @Html.ValidationMessageFor(model => model.LastName, "",
                      new { @class = "text-danger" })
        </div>
      </div>

      <div class="form-group">
        @Html.LabelFor(model => model.Biography, htmlAttributes:
                  new { @class = "control-label col-md-2" })
        <div class="col-md-10">
          @Html.EditorFor(model => model.Biography, new { htmlAttributes =
                      new { @class = "form-control",
                          data_bind = "value: author.biography" } })
          @Html.ValidationMessageFor(model => model.Biography, "",
                      new { @class = "text-danger" })
        </div>
      </div>

      <div class="form-group">
        <div class="col-md-offset-2 col-md-10" data-bind="visible: !sending()">
```

```
            <input type="submit" value="@if (isCreating) {
                        @Html.Raw("Create")
                    } else { @Html.Raw("Update") }"
                    class="btn btn-default" />
        </div>

        <div class="progress" data-bind="visible: sending">
            <div class="progress-bar progress-bar-info progress-bar-striped active"
                role="progressbar" aria-valuenow="100"
                aria-valuemin="0" aria-valuemax="100"
                style="width: 100%">
            <span class="sr-only"></span>
            </div>
        </div>
      </div>
    </div>
  }
</div>

<div>
  @Html.ActionLink("Back to List", "Index")
</div>

@section Scripts {
  @Scripts.Render("~/bundles/jqueryval",
      "/Scripts/ViewModels/AuthorFormViewModel.js")
  <script>
    var viewModel = new AuthorFormViewModel(@Html.HtmlConvertToJson(Model));
    ko.applyBindings(viewModel);
  </script>
}
```

Example 6-10 is an updated `AuthorFormViewModel`. It does similar things to the view by determining whether the author is being added or edited to perform minor conditional differences.

Example 6-10. AuthorFormViewModel

```
function AuthorFormViewModel(author) {
  var self = this;

  self.saveCompleted = ko.observable(false);
  self.sending = ko.observable(false);

  self.isCreating = author.id == 0;

  self.author = {
    id: author.id,
    firstName: ko.observable(author.firstName),
    lastName: ko.observable(author.lastName),
    biography: ko.observable(author.biography),
```

```
  };

  self.validateAndSave = function (form) {
    if (!$(form).valid())
      return false;

    self.sending(true);

    // include the anti forgery token
    self.author.__RequestVerificationToken = form[0].value;

    $.ajax({
      url: (self.isCreating) ? 'Create' : 'Edit',
      type: 'post',
      contentType: 'application/x-www-form-urlencoded',
      data: ko.toJS(self.author)
    })
    .success(self.successfulSave)
    .error(self.errorSave)
    .complete(function () { self.sending(false) });
  };

  self.successfulSave = function () {
    self.saveCompleted(true);

    $('.body-content').prepend(
        '<div class="alert alert-success">
        <strong>Success!</strong> The author has been saved.</div>');
    setTimeout(function () {
      if (self.isCreating)
        location.href = './';
      else
        location.href = '../';
    }, 1000);
  };

  self.errorSave = function () {
    $('.body-content').prepend(
        '<div class="alert alert-danger">
        <strong>Error!</strong> There was an error saving the author.</div>');
  };
}
```

The id is now added to the author object. It is not an observable property because it won't change during the lifetime of the request. This is used by the Edit method to indicate which author is being edited. Similar to the view, a variable called isCreat ing is defined to place the logic identifying whether the author is being added or edited. This variable is used within the validateAndSave function to change the URL of the AJAX request. When isCreating is true, it will continue to go to the Create method. When it is false, it will change and go to the Edit action. This variable is also used in the successfulSave function to properly redirect back to the authors listing page.

Both the successful and error messages have been updated to remove the word *creating* and replace it with *saving*. This could also be updated to leverage the isCreating variable; however, I like the ambiguous term of "saving."

Creating Observables

In Example 6-9, the id property in the author variable was not created as an observable. Because Knockout needs to track changes to all observables, it's important to be conscientious of how many observables get created. My general rule of thumb is, if the user cannot change it and if the UI doesn't require updating if it is changed via code, then it doesn't need to be observed. If either of these are true, then it probably should be an observed property.

It's quite common in JavaScript for variables and property names to be camelCased. I like to follow this rule when I can. As part of the Json.Net library, a data annotation is available that lets us do exactly that. The C# properties can remain PascalCase, and the JavaScript can be camelCased. Example 6-11 contains an updated Author model reflecting this.

Example 6-11. Updated Author model

```csharp
using Newtonsoft.Json;
using System;
using System.Collections.Generic;
using System.ComponentModel.DataAnnotations;
using System.Linq;
using System.Web;

namespace BootstrapIntroduction.Models
{
  public class Author
  {
    [JsonProperty(PropertyName="id")]
    public int Id { get; set; }

    [Required]
    [JsonProperty(PropertyName = "firstName")]
    public string FirstName { get; set; }

    [Required]
    [JsonProperty(PropertyName = "lastName")]
    public string LastName { get; set; }

    [JsonProperty(PropertyName = "biography")]
```

```
    public string Biography { get; set; }

    [JsonProperty(PropertyName = "books")]
    public virtual ICollection<Book> Books { get; set; }
  }
}
```

The change to the Author model now breaks the previous data bindings in the authors Index view and should be updated as shown in Example 6-12.

Example 6-12. Updated Index view

```
@using BootstrapIntroduction.Models
@model IEnumerable<Author>

@{
  ViewBag.Title = "Authors";
  var queryOptions = (QueryOptions)ViewBag.QueryOptions;
}

<h2>Authors</h2>

<p>@Html.ActionLink("Create New", "Create")</p>

<table class="table table-bordered table-striped">
  <thead>
    <tr>
      <th>@Html.BuildSortableLink("First Name", "Index", "firstName"
        , queryOptions)</th>
      <th>@Html.BuildSortableLink("Last Name", "Index", "lastName"
        , queryOptions)</th>
      <th>Actions</th>
    </tr>
  </thead>
  <tbody data-bind="foreach: authors">
    <tr>
      <td data-bind="text: firstName"></td>
      <td data-bind="text: lastName"></td>
      <td>
        <a data-bind="attr: { href: '@Url.Action("Details")/' + id }"
                 class="btn btn-info">Details</a>
        <a data-bind="attr: { href: '@Url.Action("Edit")/' + id }"
                 class="btn btn-primary">Edit</a>
        <a data-bind="attr: { href: '@Url.Action("Delete")/' + id }"
                 class="btn btn-danger">Delete</a>
      </td>
    </tr>
  </tbody>
</table>

@Html.BuildNextPreviousLinks(queryOptions, "Index")
```

```
@section Scripts {
  <script>
    function ViewModel(authors) {
      var self = this;

      self.authors = authors;
    };

    var viewModel = new ViewModel(@Html.HtmlConvertToJson(Model));
    ko.applyBindings(viewModel);
  </script>
}
```

The required changes are now completed, and the `Create` and `Edit` actions are now sharing the same View and ViewModel.

Deleting with a Modal

The scaffolded delete functionality is quite nice. I like that it contains a confirmation page allowing the users to back out and change their mind. However, I do not like the fact that users are redirected to a new page for this simple option. This section will demonstrate how to implement the same functionality within a modal window (shown in Figure 6-2).

Converting the existing functionality into a modal involves a few different steps:

1. The delete button in the *Views/Authors/Index.cshtml* view needs to change from a regular link to a Knockout `click` data binding.
2. The resulting click event from the delete button will be implemented in the `authors` ViewModel to fetch the existing delete confirmation page and display it with a Bootstrap modal.
3. To avoid adding additional markup to the `Index` view, the scaffolded *Views/ Authors/Delete.cshtml* view has been updated to contain the required markup for a Bootstrap modal.
4. The previous inline ViewModel has been moved into a new `AuthorIndexViewMo del` inside the newly created `ViewModels` folder for better code organization.

Two changes are required in the authors `Index` view. First, the delete link needs updating to include the new `click` data binding. This data binding accepts a function that will be executed by Knockout when the user clicks this button. This is shown in Example 6-13.

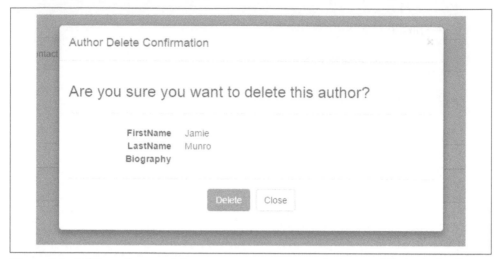

Figure 6-2. Delete author modal

Example 6-13. Updated delete button

```
<a data-bind="
  click: $parent.showDeleteModal, attr: { href: '@Url.Action("Delete")/' + id }"
  class="btn btn-danger">Delete</a>
```

Because this code is inside a Knockout `foreach` binding, the function to be called is prefixed with `$parent`. When you are inside a `foreach` binding, you are no longer in the context of the ViewModel. In this example, you are now in the context of an individual author object and only its properties are available. Knockout provides the ability to access other properties outside the current context with `$parent`.

The second change (shown in Example 6-14) updates the `Scripts` section at the bottom of the view. Previously, the ViewModel was contained in the view. It has now been moved to a new file called `AuthorIndexViewModel`. This file is included and then instantiated with the list of authors as before.

Example 6-14. Updated Scripts section

```
@section Scripts {
  @Scripts.Render("/Scripts/ViewModels/AuthorIndexViewModel.js")
  <script>
    var viewModel = new AuthorIndexViewModel(@Html.HtmlConvertToJson(Model));
    ko.applyBindings(viewModel);
  </script>
}
```

Example 6-15 contains the enhanced `AuthorIndexViewModel`. It contains two new functions: `showDeleteModal` and `deleteAuthor`.

Example 6-15. New AuthorIndexViewModel

```
function AuthorIndexViewModel(authors) {
  var self = this;

  self.authors = authors;

  self.showDeleteModal = function (data, event) {
    self.sending = ko.observable(false);

    $.get($(event.target).attr('href'), function (d) {
      $('.body-content').prepend(d);
      $('#deleteModal').modal('show');

      ko.applyBindings(self, document.getElementById('deleteModal'));
    });
  };

  self.deleteAuthor = function (form) {
    self.sending(true);
    return true;
  };
};
```

The `showDeleteModal` function is called when the user clicks the delete button. It contains two parameters: `data` and `event`. The `data` parameter contains the current author with all of its properties. The second parameter, `event`, contains the HTML element that the click binding is attached to. This parameter is used in the AJAX call to specify the URL of the request.

When the AJAX request completes, the resulting HTML is prepended to the body-content class. Once the HTML is prepended, the modal is shown to the user by accessing the newly added HTML element with the `id` of `deleteModal` and calling the modal with the value of `show`.

The updated `Delete` view (shown in Example 6-16) contains a couple of Knockout bindings. For these to be processed by Knockout, the `ko.applyBindings` needs to be executed with a ViewModel—in this case, the current ViewModel. An optional second parameter is provided that limits the scope of the binding to the newly inserted delete modal.

The `deleteAuthor` function is called when the user confirms the deletion of the author. This function sets the sending observable that was created in the `showDelete Modal` to true. In the delete modal, this will hide the submit button options. The function returns true, so the form will be submitted as usual. Normally, Knockout automatically returns false to prevent the submission of the form.

Example 6-16 contains an updated `Delete` view. The initial view contained a preview of the author being deleted and the creation of a new form with a submit button to delete. This has been maintained, but the markup is now wrapped within a modal.

Example 6-16. Updated Delete view

```
@model BootstrapIntroduction.Models.Author
@{
  ViewBag.Title = "Delete";
  Layout = null;
}

<div class="modal fade" id="deleteModal">
  <div class="modal-dialog">
    <div class="modal-content">
      <div class="modal-header">
        <button type="button" class="close" data-dismiss="modal">
                  <span aria-hidden="true">&times;</span>
                  <span class="sr-only">Close</span>
              </button>
        <h4 class="modal-title">Author Delete Confirmation</h4>
      </div>
      <div class="modal-body">
        <h3>Are you sure you want to delete this author?</h3>
        <div>
          <hr />
          <dl class="dl-horizontal">
            <dt>
              @Html.DisplayNameFor(model => model.FirstName)
            </dt>

            <dd>
              @Html.DisplayFor(model => model.FirstName)
            </dd>

            <dt>
              @Html.DisplayNameFor(model => model.LastName)
            </dt>

            <dd>
              @Html.DisplayFor(model => model.LastName)
            </dd>

            <dt>
              @Html.DisplayNameFor(model => model.Biography)
            </dt>

            <dd>
```

```
                @Html.DisplayFor(model => model.Biography)
            </dd>

        </dl>
    </div>
    <div class="modal-footer">
        @using (Html.BeginForm("Delete", "Authors", FormMethod.Post,
                    new { data_bind = "submit: deleteAuthor" }))
        {
            @Html.AntiForgeryToken()

            <div class="form-actions no-color text-center"
                        data-bind="visible: !sending()">
                <input type="submit" value="Delete" class="btn btn-danger" />
                <button type="button" class="btn btn-default"
                            data-dismiss="modal">Close</button>
            </div>

            <div class="progress" data-bind="visible: sending">
                <div class="progress-bar progress-bar-info progress-bar-striped active"
                    role="progressbar" aria-valuenow="100"
                    aria-valuemin="0" aria-valuemax="100"
                    style="width: 100%">
                    <span class="sr-only"></span>
                </div>
            </div>
        }
    </div>
    </div><!-- /.modal-content -->
  </div><!-- /.modal-dialog -->
</div><!-- /.modal -->
</div>
```

Creating a modal consists of including a wrapper div with the class of modal. The modal is then divided into three separate sections: the header, the body, and the footer. In the delete modal, the header contains a title indicating that the user needs to confirm the deletion of this author. The body contains the preview of the author's information. And the footer contains the form that will submit the author for deletion.

This form has been updated to include the submit data binding, which calls the aforementioned deleteAuthor function. The progress bar that was included when adding or editing an author is also included here and shown once the user has clicked the delete button.

Once the user clicks the delete button, it performs a regular form post. In the Author sController, the results of a successful author deletion redirect the user back to the authors listing page. This will hide the modal and cause the list of authors to be updated with the deleted author removed.

Empty Table Listings

Once I started to delete and add authors, I noticed that an empty table is shown when there are zero authors. Also, because there are Knockout data bindings contained within the first table, there is a flicker of an empty table row and buttons. This, of course, looks a little awkward.

This next example will solve it by applying a `visible` binding to the table. An alert message will also be shown when there are no authors. Example 6-17 contains an updated *Views/Authors/Index.cshtml* views with the subtle changes.

Example 6-17. Updated Authors view

```
@using BootstrapIntroduction.Models
@model IEnumerable<Author>

@{
  ViewBag.Title = "Authors";
  var queryOptions = (QueryOptions)ViewBag.QueryOptions;
}

<h2>Authors</h2>

<p>@Html.ActionLink("Create New", "Create")</p>

<div style="display: none" data-bind="visible: authors.length > 0">
  <table class="table table-bordered table-striped">
    <thead>
      <tr>
        <th>@Html.BuildSortableLink("First Name", "Index", "firstName"
            , queryOptions)</th>
        <th>@Html.BuildSortableLink("Last Name", "Index", "lastName"
            , queryOptions)</th>
        <th>Actions</th>
      </tr>
    </thead>
    <tbody data-bind="foreach: authors">
      <tr>
        <td data-bind="text: firstName"></td>
        <td data-bind="text: lastName"></td>
        <td>
          <a data-bind="attr: { href: '@Url.Action("Details")/' + id }"
                      class="btn btn-info">Details</a>
          <a data-bind="attr: { href: '@Url.Action("Edit")/' + id }"
                      class="btn btn-primary">Edit</a>
          <a data-bind="click: $parent.showDeleteModal,
                      attr: { href: '@Url.Action("Delete")/' + id }"
                      class="btn btn-danger">Delete</a>
        </td>
      </tr>
```

```
      </tbody>
    </table>

    @Html.BuildNextPreviousLinks(queryOptions, "Index")
</div>

<div style="display: none" data-bind="visible: authors.length == 0"
   class="alert alert-warning alert-dismissible" role="alert">
   <button type="button" class="close" data-dismiss="alert">
      <span aria-hidden="true">&times;</span>
      <span class="sr-only">Close</span>
   </button>
   There are no authors to display.
   Click @Html.ActionLink("here", "Create") to create one now.
</div>

@section Scripts {
   @Scripts.Render("/Scripts/ViewModels/AuthorIndexViewModel.js")
   <script>
      var viewModel = new AuthorIndexViewModel(@Html.HtmlConvertToJson(Model));
      ko.applyBindings(viewModel);
   </script>
}
```

The table and pagination links are now wrapped in a `div` tag. This `div` contains a data binding that will make it hidden when the length of the authors array is 0. There is also an inline style of `display: none` on this element. This means by default it will be hidden until the Knockout bindings are executed.

An alert message has also been added (as shown in Figure 6-3). The `div` tag for the alert contains the inverse data binding, meaning that it will only be shown when there are no authors; otherwise, it will remain hidden. This `div` also contains an inline style with `display: none`.

Figure 6-3. Empty authors listing

Without the inline style to make both elements hidden by default, prior to Knockout being executed and hiding one of the two properties, both would be temporarily visible to the user. The side effect of this is that the page will be temporarily empty until Knockout executes the data bindings and shows the appropriate element. I prefer the empty page look to the on and off flicker of elements.

Summary

Chapter 5 provided the ability to add, edit, delete, and view the authors in the database. It introduced some nice functionality on the index page to sort and page through the authors. This chapter focused on the managing portion of it. The add and edit forms were updated to share the view and ViewModel and submit the author via AJAX. The delete was then updated to show the confirmation in a modal instead of going to a new page to perform the delete confirmation.

As a good learning exercise, I would suggest that you attempt the same changes on the Books table. Begin by scaffolding a `BooksController` and then perform the similar steps completed throughout this chapter and Chapter 5.

CHAPTER 7

Server-Side ViewModels

Chapter 3 introduced client-side ViewModels that are used to perform data bindings with Knockout. I would consider them identical in purpose, but they live at a different level in the lifecycle of a web request.

A server-side ViewModel is generated from a data model. The ViewModel is then bound to a view. In Chapter 5 and Chapter 6 when the `AuthorsController` was scaffolded from the `Author` model, the `Author` model is also being used as a ViewModel for the various views in the CRUD operation.

In Chapter 6, client-side ViewModels were created that accepted the ViewModel from the Razor view (the data model), and they were bound to the view via Knockout. The major difference between client-side and server-side ViewModels is that server-side ViewModels are static. Once the web request has been returned from the server to the client, the server-side ViewModel will never change, whereas the client-side ViewModel is dynamic and responds to user interactions on the web page.

Why Create Server-Side ViewModels?

This is an important question. As you will see very soon, when I create an Authors ViewModel, it will be nearly identical to the Authors model, so why should we create them?

In Chapter 5, when the `AuthorsController` was first scaffolded from the `Author` model, the list of authors was serialized to JSON and provided to the client-side ViewModel. If you view the source of the authors index page, you will notice the list of books for each author was also serialized. I consider this a mistake because unnecessary data was transferred to the client, and this data was then unnecessarily bound to the ViewModel.

The definition of a ViewModel is to bind data from a model so that it can be accessed easily by a view. Returning the unneeded and unused array of books breaks this definition. This, of course, is required by the data model and Entity Framework to create inter-relationships.

It is also quite common for data models to contain nonpublic data. For example, an Authors table may often contain contact information that should not be displayed publicly, but be available for internal use. These fields would exist in the data model, but they would not exist in the ViewModel.

The concept of a server-side ViewModel could have existed in Chapter 3 with the Person model that demonstrated how Knockout ViewModels accepted input. In this case, the Person is a not a data model, but rather it is a ViewModel used for the `Advanced` view in the `HomeController`.

Chapter 5 also introduced two additional ViewModels that at the time were placed in the *Models* directory: `QueryOptions` and `SortOrder`. These also do not correspond to data models; they are used by the View and the Controller to communicate information back and forth.

With a good understanding of server-side ViewModels, it is a good time to create a new *ViewModels* folder in the root of the project. The `Person`, `QueryOptions`, and `SortOrder` classes should then be relocated to this folder.

ViewModels Namespace

When you relocate the preceding three classes, it is a good idea to adjust the namespaces. Because these classes were created inside the *Models* directory, their namespace is `BootstrapIntroduc` `tion.Models`. An updated namespace would be to change it to `BootstrapIntroduction.ViewModels`. Once you update the namespace in the class, you'll need to update any reference to it and include the newly named namespace, for example the `HomeCon` `troller`, the `HtmlHelperExtension`, the *Advanced.cshtml*, etc.

It's not necessary to update the namespace; however, if your project continues to grow and you create a Person data model, you would receive an error because a `Person` class would already exist in that namespace.

Going forward, Controllers will now be responsible for converting Models to ViewModels for output, and vice versa for input (as shown in Figure 7-1). The remainder of this chapter will update the `AuthorsController` to demonstrate this.

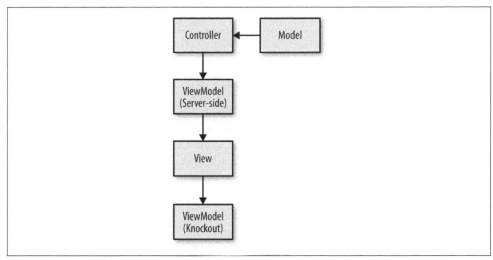

Figure 7-1. Server-side ViewModels

The Authors ViewModel

Example 7-1 creates a new class called `AuthorViewModel` inside the newly created *ViewModels* directory. Even though the class is contained within the *ViewModels* folder, I do like post-fixing ViewModel in the name because it helps to easily distinguish the ViewModel from the data model.

Example 7-1. AuthorViewModel

```
using Newtonsoft.Json;
using System;
using System.Collections.Generic;
using System.ComponentModel.DataAnnotations;
using System.Linq;
using System.Web;

namespace BootstrapIntroduction.ViewModels
{
  public class AuthorViewModel
  {
    [JsonProperty(PropertyName="id")]
    public int Id { get; set; }

    [Required]
    [JsonProperty(PropertyName = "firstName")]
    public string FirstName { get; set; }

    [Required]
    [JsonProperty(PropertyName = "lastName")]
```

```
    public string LastName { get; set; }

    [JsonProperty(PropertyName = "biography")]
    public string Biography { get; set; }
  }
}
```

The `AuthorViewModel` is nearly identical to the Author data model. It contains the `JsonProperty` annotations because this model will now be serialized for the Java-Script ViewModels. It also contains the validation annotations because, as will be demonstrated in a later section, the add and edit forms will be using this model in the form. Adding the data validation will allow the form to ensure the appropriate fields are populated.

Updating the Authors Listing

Updating the list of authors to use the new `AuthorViewModel` requires two changes:

1. Update the *Index.cshtml* to be bound to a list of `AuthorViewModels` instead of Author model.
2. Update the `AuthorsController` to convert the list of `Author` models to a list of `AuthorViewModels`.

Updating the authors *Index.cshtml* requires changes to the first two lines of the entire view, as shown in Example 7-2.

Example 7-2. Changing to AuthorViewModel

```
@using BootstrapIntroduction.ViewModels
@model IEnumerable<AuthorViewModel>
```

Converting the list of models to ViewModels is equally as easy because I am going to leverage a new third-party library called *Automapper*. Automapper is a library that lets you define a map from the source (Author data model) to a destination (`Author ViewModel`). It will automatically go through each record in the list, and all properties that are named the same will be copied from the source to the destination.

Automapper can also be customized to map properties that don't match in name with a little bit of configuration. That's not necessary at this time, however, because the naming conventions between the `Author` model and `AuthorViewModel` are identical.

To install Automapper, right-click the project and select Manage NuGet Packages. With the Online option selected on the left, search for Automapper. Click the Install button on the first result.

Using Automapper in code requires two things. The first is to define the mapping that identifies the source class and the destination class. The second is to run the map. Example 7-3 shows an updated `Index` function inside the `AuthorsController`.

Example 7-3. Updated AuthorsController Index

```
public ActionResult Index([Form] QueryOptions queryOptions)
{
  var start = (queryOptions.CurrentPage - 1) * queryOptions.PageSize;

  var authors = db.Authors.
    OrderBy(queryOptions.Sort).
    Skip(start).
    Take(queryOptions.PageSize);

  queryOptions.TotalPages =
    (int)Math.Ceiling((double)db.Authors.Count() / queryOptions.PageSize);

  ViewBag.QueryOptions = queryOptions;

  AutoMapper.Mapper.CreateMap<Author, AuthorViewModel>();

  return View(AutoMapper.Mapper.Map<List<Author>,
                  List<AuthorViewModel>>(authors.ToList()));
}
```

The two Automapper lines appear almost identical; the first one calls a `CreateMap` function, and the second calls the `Map` function. The second line also defines the source and destination slightly differently. When the Automapper map is defined, it only takes the class names; however, if you want to convert an entire collection of those models, you must indicate that when calling the `Map` function.

The listing of authors is now data bound to a ViewModel instead of a data model.

Updating the Add/Edit Form

Updating the add and edit authors form involves the same two things as updating the index. The authors *Form.cshtml* view needs to be data bound to the `AuthorViewModel` (as shown in Example 7-4).

Example 7-4. Updated Authors Form

```
@model BootstrapIntroduction.ViewModels.AuthorViewModel
```

The `AuthorsController` then needs to be updated to convert the data. The `Index` function only has to convert from the data model to the ViewModel; for the add and edit form, it also needs to convert from the ViewModel to the data model. Example 7-5 contains updates to both of the Create and both of the Edit functions.

Example 7-5. Updated AuthorsController

```
// GET: Authors/Create
public ActionResult Create()
{
  return View("Form", new AuthorViewModel());
}

// POST: Authors/Create
[HttpPost]
[ValidateAntiForgeryToken]
public ActionResult Create([Bind(Include = "Id,FirstName,LastName,Biography")]
                AuthorViewModel author)
{
  if (ModelState.IsValid)
  {
    AutoMapper.Mapper.CreateMap<AuthorViewModel, Author>();
    db.Authors.Add(AutoMapper.Mapper.Map<AuthorViewModel, Author>(author));
    db.SaveChanges();
    return RedirectToAction("Index");
  }

  return View(author);
}

// GET: Authors/Edit/5
public ActionResult Edit(int? id)
{
  if (id == null)
  {
    return new HttpStatusCodeResult(HttpStatusCode.BadRequest);
  }
  Author author = db.Authors.Find(id);
  if (author == null)
  {
    return HttpNotFound();
  }

  AutoMapper.Mapper.CreateMap<Author, AuthorViewModel>();
  return View("Form", AutoMapper.Mapper.Map<Author, AuthorViewModel>(author));
}

// POST: Authors/Edit/5
[HttpPost]
[ValidateAntiForgeryToken]
public ActionResult Edit([Bind(Include = "Id,FirstName,LastName,Biography")]
                AuthorViewModel author)
{
```

```
    if (ModelState.IsValid)
    {
      AutoMapper.Mapper.CreateMap<AuthorViewModel, Author>();
      db.Entry(AutoMapper.Mapper.Map<AuthorViewModel, Author>(author)).State
                   = EntityState.Modified;
      db.SaveChanges();
      return RedirectToAction("Index");
    }

    return View("Form", author);
}
```

The first `Create` function was updated to create a new `AuthorViewModel` instead of the previous `Author` data model.

The second `Create` function (that is called when the form is posted) was updated to implement the Automapper. This time the source is the `AuthorViewModel` and the destination is the `Author` data model.

The first `Edit` function was updated to be similar to the `Index` function. It uses Automapper to convert from the data model to the ViewModel. This will allow the form to be prepopulated with the existing author data from the database.

The second `Edit` function (also called when the form is posted) was updated just like the second `Create` function to perform the conversion from the `AuthorViewModel` to the `Author` data model. This allows the updated `Author` to be saved to the database.

Updating the Delete Modal

You guessed it! Updating the deletion of an author requires the same two updates. First, the *Delete.cshtml* file needs to be updated to the `AuthorViewModel` as shown in Example 7-6.

Example 7-6. Updated Delete Author view

```
@model BootstrapIntroduction.ViewModels.AuthorViewModel
```

The `Delete` function in the `AuthorsController` needs to be updated just like the first `Edit` function. It creates an Automapper from the data model to the ViewModel as shown in Example 7-7.

Example 7-7. Updated Delete AuthorsController

```
public ActionResult Delete(int? id)
{
  if (id == null)
  {
```

```
      return new HttpStatusCodeResult(HttpStatusCode.BadRequest);
   }
   Author author = db.Authors.Find(id);
   if (author == null)
   {
      return HttpNotFound();
   }
   AutoMapper.Mapper.CreateMap<Author, AuthorViewModel>();
   return View(AutoMapper.Mapper.Map<Author, AuthorViewModel>(author));
}
```

The second `Delete` function requires no updates because it doesn't accept the entire `Author` model as input when the delete is confirmed; it simply accepts the `id`. The `id` is used to fetch the author and delete it from the database. It also does not return the `Author` model (because it was just deleted).

Summary

Implementing server-side ViewModels can appear as duplicated code to the data model, and I sometimes feel this way. However, as soon as you have a single property or relationship that is not required by the View, ViewModels become almost mandatory.

The next chapter will introduce Web API, for which ViewModels are a prerequisite because models are often the view in the Web API. Data models that contain a circular relationship (an author can have many books and a book has one author is a circular relationship) cannot be used in the return.

CHAPTER 8

Introduction to Web API

Web API was briefly mentioned in Chapter 1 because Visual Studio provides a template for automatically creating a Web API application. Web API allows you to build RESTful (*http://en.wikipedia.org/wiki/Representational_state_transfer*) web applications. When using Web API in combination with the MVC architecture pattern, the *Controller* is often the entry point for the *Resource* (Model) being interacted with. The View with Web API is often a JSON or XML representation of the resource.

This chapter will demonstrate the Web API by enhancing the CRUD interaction with the authors that the previous two chapters have been focusing on. In this chapter, the listing of authors will be updated to perform the sorting and paging of authors via a Web API controller. Likewise, adding and editing an author will also interact with the same Web API controller. Previously, new HTML pages were returned, but when Web API is integrated, the HTML will be updated to use Knockout data bindings. These will be dynamically updated by the result of an AJAX request to a Web API endpoint, which will prevent full-page reloads.

Installing Web API

In Chapter 1, when the BootstrapIntroduction project was first created, Web API was not included. This means it now needs to be added via the NuGet Package Manager. If you wish to avoid the visual NuGet Package Manager, a console utility is also available. To install packages via the console, click Tools → NuGet Package Manager → Package Manager Console. In the console window, enter **Install-Package Micro soft.AspNet.WebApi** to install the Web API package.

When a new project is created with Web API, Visual Studio scaffolds several additional pieces that, when installed via the NuGet Package Manager, are not set up. Let's configure those now.

Example 8-1 is a new file called *WebApiConfig* and should be added to the *App_Start* folder. This file is very similar to the *RouteConfig* that was explored in Chapter 1 with the default routing.

Example 8-1. WebApiConfig

```
using System;
using System.Collections.Generic;
using System.Linq;
using System.Web.Http;

namespace BootstrapIntroduction
{
  public static class WebApiConfig
  {
    public static void Register(HttpConfiguration config)
    {
      // Web API configuration and services

      // Web API routes
      config.MapHttpAttributeRoutes();

      config.Routes.MapHttpRoute(
        name: "DefaultApi",
        routeTemplate: "api/{controller}/{id}",
        defaults: new { id = RouteParameter.Optional }
      );
    }
  }
}
```

Just like *RouteConfig*, this creates a new default route that will allow the common HTTP verbs associated with a RESTful application to work out of the box. A key difference is that all URLs are prefixed with *api* before the controller and action.

Next, in the root folder of the project, the *Global.asax.cs* file requires a minor update (as shown in Example 8-2) to configure the newly added Web API routes.

Example 8-2. Updated Global.asax.cs

```
using BootstrapIntroduction.DAL;
using System;
using System.Collections.Generic;
using System.Data.Entity;
using System.Linq;
using System.Web;
using System.Web.Http;
using System.Web.Mvc;
using System.Web.Optimization;
using System.Web.Routing;
```

```
namespace BootstrapIntroduction
{
  public class MvcApplication : System.Web.HttpApplication
  {
    protected void Application_Start()
    {
      AreaRegistration.RegisterAllAreas();
      GlobalConfiguration.Configure(WebApiConfig.Register);
      FilterConfig.RegisterGlobalFilters(GlobalFilters.Filters);
      RouteConfig.RegisterRoutes(RouteTable.Routes);
      BundleConfig.RegisterBundles(BundleTable.Bundles);

      var bookContext = new BookContext();
      Database.SetInitializer(new BookInitializer());
      bookContext.Database.Initialize(true);
    }
  }
}
```

If you create a new project and include the Web API framework at the same time, these steps are not needed because Visual Studio will automatically configure this.

And finally, a new `AuthorsController` can be created. Prior to creating the file for the new `AuthorsController`, create a new folder called *api* inside of the *Controllers* folder. Once created, right-click the new folder and add a new *Controller*. This time, select Web API 2 Controller - Empty to finish creating the empty `AuthorsController` (as shown in Example 8-3).

Example 8-3. Empty AuthorsController

```
using System;
using System.Collections.Generic;
using System.Linq;
using System.Net;
using System.Net.Http;
using System.Web.Http;

namespace BootstrapIntroduction.Controllers.Api
{
  public class AuthorsController : ApiController
  {
  }
}
```

Much like the regular MVC controllers that were created earlier, Web API controllers are classes that extend a base `ApiController` class instead of the `Controller` class. Like the `Controller` class, the `ApiController` contains a lot of core methods that will help bind and execute the custom controller code and return for output.

Updating the List of Authors

In Chapter 5, the list of authors was sorted and paged via an MVC controller. This meant that each time a link was clicked, the entire HTML would be refreshed. In this chapter, a Web API controller will be used not to return back a full HTML page, but to return only an updated list of authors with the sorting and paging applied.

The Index view will contain new Knockout bindings that will then automatically update the list of authors when the AJAX call is successfully completed.

Example 8-4 is the Web API AuthorsController with a Get function that accepts the QueryOptions as input from the URL. The code to sort the authors and page through them is identical to the MVC AuthorsController.

Example 8-4. Get AuthorsController

```
using System;
using System.Collections.Generic;
using System.Data;
using System.Data.Entity;
using System.Data.Entity.Infrastructure;
using System.Linq;
using System.Linq.Dynamic;
using System.Net;
using System.Net.Http;
using System.Web.Http;
using System.Web.Http.Description;
using BootstrapIntroduction.DAL;
using BootstrapIntroduction.Models;
using BootstrapIntroduction.ViewModels;

namespace BootstrapIntroduction.Controllers.Api
{
  public class AuthorsController : ApiController
  {
    private BookContext db = new BookContext();

    // GET: api/Authors
    public ResultList<AuthorViewModel> Get([FromUri]QueryOptions queryOptions)
    {
      var start = (queryOptions.CurrentPage - 1) * queryOptions.PageSize;

      var authors = db.Authors.
        OrderBy(queryOptions.Sort).
        Skip(start).
        Take(queryOptions.PageSize);

      queryOptions.TotalPages =
        (int)Math.Ceiling((double)db.Authors.Count() / queryOptions.PageSize);
```

```
    AutoMapper.Mapper.CreateMap<Author, AuthorViewModel>();

    return new ResultList<AuthorViewModel>
    {
      QueryOptions = queryOptions,
      Results = AutoMapper.Mapper.Map<List<Author>, List<AuthorViewModel>>
          (authors.ToList())
    };
  }

  protected override void Dispose(bool disposing)
  {
    if (disposing)
    {
      db.Dispose();
    }
    base.Dispose(disposing);
  }
 }
}
```

Example 8-4 demonstrates some immediate differences between an MVC controller
and a Web API controller. The `QueryOptions` input parameter in both controllers
comes from URL parameters; however, they are attributed differently in the controllers. An MVC controller defines it as `Form`, and a Web API controller defines it as
`FromUri`.

Second, the MVC controller would typically finish an action by returning via a call to
the `View` function. With Web API, the object that you wish to return is returned as-is.
In this example, a new class called `ResultList` (shown in Example 8-5) of type
`AuthorViewModel` is returned. Based on the request made to the Web API controller,
the results will be encoded as JSON or XML. Knockout works really well with JSON,
so that is what will be used.

Example 8-5 is a new ViewModel called `ResultList`. This class should be added to
the previously created *ViewModels* folder. This class contains a generic property
called `List<T>` that allows this class to be reused for other listing pages. In Example
8-4, the `ResultList` was created with a type of `AuthorViewModel`.

Example 8-5. ResultList ViewModel

```
using Newtonsoft.Json;
using System;
using System.Collections.Generic;
using System.Linq;
using System.Web;

namespace BootstrapIntroduction.ViewModels
{
```

```
public class ResultList<T>
{
  [JsonProperty(PropertyName="queryOptions")]
  public QueryOptions QueryOptions { get; set; }

  [JsonProperty(PropertyName = "results")]
  public List<T> Results { get; set; }
}
}
```

Along with the generic list property, the ResultList contains a second property for the QueryOptions. In Chapter 5, the QueryOptions were returned to the Index view in the ViewBag. In this example, they are bound in the ResultList ViewModel. This model will be used by Knockout to dynamically update the user interface (UI) when the authors are sorted or paged.

To make it easier to provide consistency to the Knockout ViewModel, the Index view in the original MVC AuthorsController will also be updated to leverage the new ResultList ViewModel. Example 8-6 contains an updated Index function from the AuthorsController that constructs the new ResultList ViewModel just like Example 8-4 did in the Web API AuthorsController.

Example 8-6. Index action

```
public ActionResult Index([Form] QueryOptions queryOptions)
{
  var start = (queryOptions.CurrentPage - 1) * queryOptions.PageSize;

  var authors = db.Authors.
    OrderBy(queryOptions.Sort).
    Skip(start).
    Take(queryOptions.PageSize);

  queryOptions.TotalPages =
    (int)Math.Ceiling((double)db.Authors.Count() / queryOptions.PageSize);

  AutoMapper.Mapper.CreateMap<Author, AuthorViewModel>();

  return View(new ResultList<AuthorViewModel>
  {
    QueryOptions = queryOptions,
    Results = AutoMapper.Mapper.Map<List<Author>,
                  List<AuthorViewModel>>(authors.ToList())
  });
}
```

The QueryOptions that were previously passed via the ViewBag have been moved into the ResultList ViewModel. This will force the *Index.cshtml* view to require minor changes to accomodate the new model being bound and where the `QueryOptions` are retrieved from.

Example 8-7 contains a fully updated `Index` view. It contains the previously described changes, as well as several others that implement Knockout bindings to perform the previous sorting and paging that were happening via regular HTML links. These links have been updated to generate Knockout bindings that will execute an AJAX request to the Web API and dynamically update the list of authors.

Example 8-7. Index view

```
@using BootstrapIntroduction.ViewModels
@model ResultList<AuthorViewModel>

@{
  ViewBag.Title = "Authors";
  var queryOptions = Model.QueryOptions;
}

<h2>Authors</h2>

<p>@Html.ActionLink("Create New", "Create")</p>

<div style="display: none" data-bind="visible: pagingService.entities().length > 0">
  <table class="table table-bordered table-striped">
    <thead>
      <tr>
        <th>@Html.BuildKnockoutSortableLink("First Name", "Index", "firstName")</th>
        <th>@Html.BuildKnockoutSortableLink("Last Name", "Index", "lastName")</th>
        <th>Actions</th>
      </tr>
    </thead>
    <tbody data-bind="foreach: pagingService.entities">
      <tr>
        <td data-bind="text: firstName"></td>
        <td data-bind="text: lastName"></td>
        <td>
          <a data-bind="attr: { href: '@Url.Action("Details")/' + id }"
                    class="btn btn-info">Details</a>
          <a data-bind="attr: { href: '@Url.Action("Edit")/' + id }"
                    class="btn btn-primary">Edit</a>
          <a data-bind="click: $parent.showDeleteModal,
                    attr: { href: '@Url.Action("Delete")/' + id }"
                    class="btn btn-danger">Delete</a>
        </td>
      </tr>
    </tbody>
  </table>

@Html.BuildKnockoutNextPreviousLinks("Index")
```

```
</div>

<div style="display: none" data-bind="visible: pagingService.entities().length == 0"
                    class="alert alert-warning alert-dismissible" role="alert">
  <button type="button" class="close" data-dismiss="alert">
      <span aria-hidden="true">&times;</span><span class="sr-only">Close</span>
  </button>
  There are no authors to display. Click @Html.ActionLink("here", "Create")
      to create one now.
</div>

@section Scripts {
  @Scripts.Render("/Scripts/Services/PagingService.js",
                    "/Scripts/ViewModels/AuthorIndexViewModel.js")
  <script>
    var viewModel = new AuthorIndexViewModel(@Html.HtmlConvertToJson(Model));
    ko.applyBindings(viewModel);
  </script>
}
```

This code will not compile just yet because new files and HtmlHelper extensions need to be created. Prior to reviewing those, let's go through the several important changes to the Index view.

First, there was an array of authors contained in the Knockout ViewModel. This has been replaced with a new observableArray called entities under the pagingSer vice object. The pagingService is a new JavaScript class that can be reused across different HTML views to allow easy paging and sorting of your data. The entities is an observableArray, which means whenever this array changes, Knockout will automatically update any data bindings that reference it. When changing the sort order, the list of authors will be dynamically redrawn with the results of the AJAX call from the Web API controller.

Next, the previously created HtmlHelper extension methods that helped build the sortable link and the next/previous page links have been updated to call a new method. They contain the same name with Knockout injected after the word Build to identify that these methods will build Knockout-specific links.

The final change in the Index view is that the Scripts.Render call has been updated to include the new PagingService file that will be created in Example 8-9.

Example 8-8 contains the newly created HtmlHelper extension methods that create the Knockout data-bound links for sorting and paging.

Example 8-8. HtmlHelperExtension

```
using BootstrapIntroduction.ViewModels;
using Newtonsoft.Json;
```

```csharp
using System.Web;
using System.Web.Mvc;
using System.Web.Mvc.Html;

public static class HtmlHelperExtensions
{
    // other functions removed for an abbreviated example

    public static MvcHtmlString BuildKnockoutSortableLink(this HtmlHelper htmlHelper,
        string fieldName, string actionName, string sortField)
    {
        var urlHelper = new UrlHelper(htmlHelper.ViewContext.RequestContext);

        return new MvcHtmlString(string.Format(
            "<a href=\"{0}\" data-bind=\"click: pagingService.sortEntitiesBy\"" +
            " data-sort-field=\"{1}\">{2} " +
            "<span data-bind=\"css: pagingService.buildSortIcon('{1}')\"></span></a>",
            urlHelper.Action(actionName),
            sortField,
            fieldName));
    }

    public static MvcHtmlString BuildKnockoutNextPreviousLinks(
        this HtmlHelper htmlHelper, string actionName)
    {
        var urlHelper = new UrlHelper(htmlHelper.ViewContext.RequestContext);

        return new MvcHtmlString(string.Format(
"<nav>" +
"    <ul class=\"pager\">" +
"      <li data-bind=\"css: pagingService.buildPreviousClass()\">" +
"        <a href=\"{0}\" data-bind=\"click: pagingService.previousPage\">
            Previous</a></li>" +
"      <li data-bind=\"css: pagingService.buildNextClass()\">" +
"        <a href=\"{0}\" data-bind=\"click: pagingService.nextPage\">Next
            </a></li></li>" +
"    </ul>" +
"</nav>",
        @urlHelper.Action(actionName)
        ));
    }

    // other functions removed for an abbreviated example
}
```

These two functions are quite similar to their counterparts (the non-Knockout versions) in that they return a new MvcHtmlString to perform the sorting or paging. The non-Knockout versions leveraged the QueryOptions to construct a full URL. These functions instead leverage the Knockout click data binding. The click data binding allows you to specify a function to call inside your Knockout ViewModel.

The `BuildKnockoutSortableLink` binds the click to the `sortEntitiesBy` function within the aforementioned `PagingService` class. Inside this link, the sorting icon is leveraging another Knockout data binding called *css*. The results of the `buildSortIcon` function in the `PagingService` returns the appropriate class names to build the sort icon. The `buildSortIcon` is a `computedObservable` function, which means that when Knockout detects a change in any observed property within the function, it will re-execute the function to update what it is data bound to. This will allow for the sorting link to change each time you alter the sort order.

The `BuildKnockoutNextPreviousLinks` works quite similarly to the sortable link function. The previous and next links are data bound to the click event that calls the `previousPage` and `nextPage` functions, respectively, from the `PagingService` class. Both links also contain a `css` data binding to mark them as disabled when the previous and next links are unavailable.

Example 8-9 contains the new `PagingService` JavaScript class. For organization purposes, I have created a new *Services* folder inside of the *Scripts* folder and added the *PagingService.js* file here.

Example 8-9. PagingService

```javascript
function PagingService(resultList) {
 var self = this;
 self.queryOptions = {
   currentPage: ko.observable(),
   totalPages: ko.observable(),
   pageSize: ko.observable(),
   sortField: ko.observable(),
   sortOrder: ko.observable()
 };

 self.entities = ko.observableArray();

 self.updateResultList = function (resultList) {
   self.queryOptions.currentPage(resultList.queryOptions.currentPage);
   self.queryOptions.totalPages(resultList.queryOptions.totalPages);
   self.queryOptions.pageSize(resultList.queryOptions.pageSize);
   self.queryOptions.sortField(resultList.queryOptions.sortField);
   self.queryOptions.sortOrder(resultList.queryOptions.sortOrder);

   self.entities(resultList.results);
 };

 self.updateResultList(resultList);

 self.sortEntitiesBy = function (data, event) {
   var sortField = $(event.target).data('sortField');
```

```
  if (sortField == self.queryOptions.sortField() &&
                   self.queryOptions.sortOrder() == "ASC")
    self.queryOptions.sortOrder("DESC");
  else
    self.queryOptions.sortOrder("ASC");

  self.queryOptions.sortField(sortField);
  self.queryOptions.currentPage(1);

  self.fetchEntities(event);
};

self.previousPage = function (data, event) {
  if (self.queryOptions.currentPage() > 1) {
    self.queryOptions.currentPage(self.queryOptions.currentPage() - 1);

    self.fetchEntities(event);
  }
};

self.nextPage = function (data, event) {
  if (self.queryOptions.currentPage() < self.queryOptions.totalPages()) {
    self.queryOptions.currentPage(self.queryOptions.currentPage() + 1);

    self.fetchEntities(event);
  }
};

self.fetchEntities = function (event) {
  var url = '/api/' + $(event.target).attr('href');
  url += "?sortField=" + self.queryOptions.sortField();
  url += "&sortOrder=" + self.queryOptions.sortOrder();
  url += "&currentPage=" + self.queryOptions.currentPage();
  url += "&pageSize=" + self.queryOptions.pageSize();

  $.ajax({
    dataType: 'json',
    url: url
  }).success(function (data) {
    self.updateResultList(data);
  }).error(function () {
    $('.body-content').prepend('<div class="alert alert-danger">
        <strong>Error!</strong> There was an error fetching the data.</div>');
  });
};

self.buildSortIcon = function (sortField) {
  return ko.pureComputed(function () {
    var sortIcon = 'sort';

    if (self.queryOptions.sortField() == sortField) {
      sortIcon += '-by-alphabet';
```

```
        if (self.queryOptions.sortOrder() == "DESC")
          sortIcon += '-alt';
      }

      return 'glyphicon glyphicon-' + sortIcon;
    });
  };

  self.buildPreviousClass = ko.pureComputed(function () {
    var className = 'previous';

    if (self.queryOptions.currentPage() == 1)
      className += ' disabled';

    return className;
  });

  self.buildNextClass = ko.pureComputed(function () {
    var className = 'next';

    if (self.queryOptions.currentPage() == self.queryOptions.totalPages())
      className += ' disabled';

    return className;
  });
}
```

The PagingService class starts by creating two properties: the queryOptions and the entities array. The queryOptions makes all of its child properties observable. This will be used to dynamically update the sort icons and build the AJAX URL to update the data. The entities array will contain the list of authors.

The updateResultList function is then defined that accepts a resultList model and sets all of the observables that were just defined. This function is then immediately called afterward to populate the observables with the input parameter to the Paging Service class. This function will also be used after the AJAX calls to update all of the observables with the results from the Web API controller.

The sortEntitiesBy, previousPage, and nextPage functions are defined next. These functions update the affected queryOptions properties to perform the sorting and paging, respectively. sortEntitiesBy sets the sortOrder and sortField passed from the link that is clicked. It then resets the currentPage to 1. The previousPage and nextPage functions decrement and increment the currentPage property, respectively. Both functions also perform a check to prevent going below and above the minimum and maximum pages. And finally, all three functions call the shared fetchEntities function.

The fetchEntities function builds the URL to call using the href attribute from the link that was clicked. Then the url variable is updated to set the various queryOptions. An AJAX request is then made to the URL. On success, the updateResultList function is called with the results of the AJAX request to update the observed properties. When the properties are updated, Knockout will automatically update the sort icons, list of authors, and paging links dynamically. If an error occurs with the AJAX request, an alert is added to notify the user they should try again.

The final three functions, buildSortIcon, buildPreviousClass, and buildNext Class, are created as pureComputed functions. The buildSortIcon accesses the sort Field and sortOrder observed properties from the queryOptions variable. Whenever these properties are updated, any UI element that is data bound to the function will be redrawn with the updated results of the function. The buildPreviou sClass and buildNextClass work similarily, but they are updated whenever the cur rentPage property on the queryOptions variable is updated.

Example 8-10 is an updated AuthorIndexViewModel. The only change is that there is no longer an array of authors. Instead, a new pagingService variable is instantiated with the new PagingService class passing in the serialized resultList from the Index view.

Example 8-10. Updated AuthorIndexViewModel

```
function AuthorIndexViewModel(resultList) {
  var self = this;

  self.pagingService = new PagingService(resultList);

  self.showDeleteModal = function (data, event) {
    self.sending = ko.observable(false);

    $.get($(event.target).attr('href'), function (d) {
      $('.body-content').prepend(d);
      $('#deleteModal').modal('show');

      ko.applyBindings(self, document.getElementById('deleteModal'));
    });
  };

  self.deleteAuthor = function (form) {
    self.sending(true);
    return true;
  };
};
```

When using Knockout, I like leveraging Web API controllers to return back only JSON data instead of the full HTML to build the list of authors. Knockout makes it really simple to dynamically update the UI by data binding to observable properties, arrays, or computed functions.

Updating the Add/Edit Authors Form

Updating the add and edit is much simpler than updating the list of authors. Most of the effort in the previous section was about maintaining the user interface. This is not required for the add and edit form, because on success, the user was redirected back to the list of authors, and on error, an alert message was dynamically added.

That will remain the same. The minor updates in the JavaScript ViewModel will involve updating the AJAX request type and changing the `contentType` (shown in Example 8-11). The rest will remain the same on the JavaScript side of things.

The MVC controller that was scaffolded in Chapter 5 will be updated to remove the automatically generated form post version of the `Create` and `Edit` actions. Similar actions will be created in the Authors Web API controller.

Example 8-11 contains an updated `validateAndSave` function from the `AuthorForm ViewModel`. It removes the previous inline `if` statement for the URL and moves it to the AJAX request type property. The `contentType` is changed from a standard form post to be of type `application/json`. The data property has been updated to leverage the similar `ko.toJS` to be `ko.toJSON`. It works quite similarily to the former, but it encodes the JavaScript variable into valid JSON to send to the server.

Example 8-11. Updated validateAndSave function

```
self.validateAndSave = function (form) {
  if (!$(form).valid())
    return false;

  self.sending(true);

  // include the anti forgery token
  self.author.__RequestVerificationToken = form[0].value;

  $.ajax({
    url: '/api/authors',
    type: (self.isCreating) ? 'post' : 'put',
    contentType: 'application/json',
    data: ko.toJSON(self.author)
  })
  .success(self.successfulSave)
  .error(self.errorSave)
  .complete(function () { self.sending(false); });
};
```

Previously, when an author was being created, the AJAX request was going to a different URL than when the author was being edited. When interacting with a RESTful API, the URL stays consistent; instead, the request type changes. When you are adding, the type is *post*. When you are editing, the request type is changed to a *put*. Similarily, if you were to implement a delete action, the request type would be *delete* and the URL would remain the same.

Example 8-12 is an updated Authors Web API controller. Two new functions `Post` and `Put` have been added that accept the `AuthorViewModel` as input.

Example 8-12. Updated Web API AuthorsController

```
using System;
using System.Collections.Generic;
using System.Data;
using System.Data.Entity;
using System.Data.Entity.Infrastructure;
using System.Linq;
using System.Linq.Dynamic;
using System.Net;
using System.Net.Http;
using System.Web.Http;
using System.Web.Http.Description;
using BootstrapIntroduction.DAL;
using BootstrapIntroduction.Models;
using BootstrapIntroduction.ViewModels;

namespace BootstrapIntroduction.Controllers.Api
{
  public class AuthorsController : ApiController
  {
    private BookContext db = new BookContext();

    // GET: api/Authors
    public ResultList<AuthorViewModel> Get([FromUri]QueryOptions queryOptions)
    {
      var start = (queryOptions.CurrentPage - 1) * queryOptions.PageSize;

      var authors = db.Authors.
        OrderBy(queryOptions.Sort).
        Skip(start).
        Take(queryOptions.PageSize);

      queryOptions.TotalPages =
        (int)Math.Ceiling((double)db.Authors.Count() / queryOptions.PageSize);

      AutoMapper.Mapper.CreateMap<Author, AuthorViewModel>();

      return new ResultList<AuthorViewModel>
      {
```

```
        QueryOptions = queryOptions,
        Results = AutoMapper.Mapper.Map<List<Author>, List<AuthorViewModel>>
            (authors.ToList())
    };
  }


  // PUT: api/Authors/5
  [ResponseType(typeof(void))]
  public IHttpActionResult Put(AuthorViewModel author)
  {
    if (!ModelState.IsValid)
    {
      return BadRequest(ModelState);
    }

    AutoMapper.Mapper.CreateMap<AuthorViewModel, Author>();
    db.Entry(AutoMapper.Mapper.Map<AuthorViewModel, Author>(author)).State
                    = EntityState.Modified;

    db.SaveChanges();

    return StatusCode(HttpStatusCode.NoContent);
  }

  // POST: api/Authors
  [ResponseType(typeof(AuthorViewModel))]
  public IHttpActionResult Post(AuthorViewModel author)
  {
    if (!ModelState.IsValid)
    {
      return BadRequest(ModelState);
    }

    AutoMapper.Mapper.CreateMap<AuthorViewModel, Author>();
    db.Authors.Add(AutoMapper.Mapper.Map<AuthorViewModel, Author>(author));
    db.SaveChanges();

    return CreatedAtRoute("DefaultApi", new { id = author.Id }, author);
  }

  protected override void Dispose(bool disposing)
  {
    if (disposing)
    {
      db.Dispose();
    }
    base.Dispose(disposing);
  }
 }
}
```

These functions are almost identical to the scaffolded MVC `AuthorsController` in that they use `AutoMapper` to convert the ViewModel to a data model and save it using the Entity Framework `DbContext`.

The key difference is that neither function returns an HTML view. The `Put` function returns an empty result and sets the HTTP Status Code to `NoContent`. The `Post` function returns an updated `AuthorViewModel` with the `id` property set with the newly created value from the database.

HTTP Status Codes

RESTful applications rely heavily on HTTP Status Codes to provide the integrator with feedback of the API request. Three main levels are commonly used:

Successful 2xx

> The common successful requests are 200 OK, 201 Created, and 204 No Content. Any request in the 200s is used to identify that the API request was successful.

Client Error 4xx

> The common client error requests are 400 Bad Request (the input data was not valid), 401 Unauthorized, 404 Not Found, and 405 Method Not Allowed. Any request in the 400s is used to identify that the API integrator is doing something incorrectly. It's quite common for the body of the response to contain a helpful error message to fix the problem prior to resubmitting the same request.

Server Error 5xx

> The common server error requests are 500 Internal Server Error, 501 Not Implemented, and 503 Service Unavailable (often used for rate-limiting the number of requests to an API). Any request in the 500s is used to identify that an error occurred on the server and the API integrator should try his request again. Similar to 400 level requests, it is quite common for the body of the response to contain a helpful error message identifying what the problem is.

To avoid unnecessary extra code, I removed the `Create` and `Edit` functions from the MVC `AuthorsController` that perform the saving of data to the database. I left the two functions that display the form to the user.

Summary

This chapter demonstrated using Web API controllers to only return JSON data from the server that gets data bound to observable Knockout properties. I think it nicely demonstrates how Knockout is capable of updating multiple UI elements when one or more observable properties are changed. It's a much smoother user interface to dynamically update the table of authors without the need for a full-page reload of the entire HTML.

If you would like to further explore Web API controllers, I would suggest that you try converting the delete modal to use two other common Web API functions. The first is an overloaded `Get (by id)` that returns an individual `AuthorViewModel` instead of a list. The second is a `Delete` method that also accepts an ID and deletes the author from the database.

Code Architecture

CHAPTER 9

Creating Global Filters

Global filters enable you to apply a consistent behavior across all requests to your web application by registering a filter during the application startup. Filters can also be applied to specific actions or entire controllers by adding an attribute to the action or controller, respectively.

Five different types of filters can be created. At the start of each web request, any filter that is defined is executed in the following order—the exception to this rule is the Exception filter (no pun intended) because these filters are only called when an error occurs:

- Authentication filters (new in MVC 5)
- Authorization filters
- Action filters
- Result filters
- Exception filters

This chapter will provide a brief overview of all five types of filters and then will demonstrate how to create Action, Result, and Exception filters. Chapter 10 will demonstrate how to create Authentication and Authorization filters.

Authentication Filters

Authentication filters are new to MVC 5. Prior to that, authentication and authorization were accomplished together in the Authorization filters. MVC 5 has now separated these two concerns.

When MVC receives a web page request, any Authentication filters will be executed first. If the request requires authentication and the user has previously been authenticated, the request will continue to the next step. If the user has not been authenticated, the request will halt processing. Based on the setup of the filter, the request may redirect the user to a login page; this is commonly done with an MVC controller. A Web API controller would more likely return a 401 Unauthorized request.

Authorization Filters

Once the request has passed any Authentication filters, the Authorization filters are executed next. The goal of an Authorization filter is to ensure that the authenticated user is allowed to access the page or resource being requested. If authorization succeeds, the request will continue to the next step. If it fails authorization, MVC controllers commonly return error pages. A Web API controller would commonly return a 403 Forbidden request. Alternatively, it may return a 404 Not Found error and inform the user that the resource being accessed does not exist, even though it actually does.

Action Filters

Action filters provide the ability to execute code at two different times. When you define an Action filter, you can optionally implement a function that executes prior to the action being requested, or optionally after the action has finished executing, but prior to generating the final results to complete the request.

Result Filters

Like Action filters, Result filters provide two different functions that can be optionally implemented. The first is when the result has finished executing; for example, in an MVC controller once the view has been fully rendered and is ready to be returned from the server. The second is when the result is executing. This function would not have access to the final content.

Exception Filters

At any time during a request being handled by MVC, any Exception filters will be executed. Filters for MVC controllers will commonly return a custom error page that can return either a specific or generic error message. Web API controllers will commonly build different HTTP status codes. For example, if the model is invalid, a 400 Bad Request could be returned. If an unknown exception occurred, a 500 error would be more appropriate to indicate a server error occurred.

Global Web API Validation

When Visual Studio scaffolds controllers and views for us, the controller contains a statement inside the `Create and Edit` methods that resembles Example 9-1.

Example 9-1. Model validation

```
if (!ModelState.IsValid)
{
  return BadRequest(ModelState);
}
```

The `ModelState` is a class that inherits from a `Dictionary` that contains key/value pairs for all of the elements in the model being validated. When the `IsValid` Boolean returns false, it indicates one or more things are invalid in the model and cannot be saved.

In a Web API controller, this means it should return a 400 Bad Request with a message indicating the issues that need to be fixed.

This section will create a new class called `ValidationActionFilterAttribute` (shown in Example 9-2). I like to organize my filters in a common folder, so I have created a new folder called *Filters* at the root of my project and created the Action filter within it.

Example 9-2. ValidationActionFilterAttribute

```
using System.Collections.Generic;
using System.Linq;
using System.Net;
using System.Net.Http;
using System.Web.Http.Controllers;
using System.Web.Http.Filters;

namespace BootstrapIntroduction.Filters
{
  public class ValidationActionFilterAttribute : ActionFilterAttribute
  {
    public override void OnActionExecuting(HttpActionContext actionContext)
    {
      var modelState = actionContext.ModelState;
      if (!modelState.IsValid)
        actionContext.Response = actionContext.Request.CreateResponse(
        HttpStatusCode.BadRequest, modelState);
    }
  }
}
```

The new Action filter inherits from the `ActionFilterAttribute`, which is an abstract class that contains four virtual functions that can be optionally overridden in your Action filter class:

OnActionExecuting

> The `OnActionExecuting` function is called just prior to executing the code inside of your controller method. As shown in Example 9-2, if the `ModelState` is invalid, the response is immediately terminated and a 400 Bad Request is returned from the server. This ensures that your data is valid when your controller method is executed based upon the validation rules of that model.

OnActionExecutingAsync

> The `OnActionExecutingAsync` function is identical to the `OnActionExecuting` function with the exception that it works with asynchronous controllers.

OnActionExecuted

> The OnActionExecuted function is called after your controller method has finished executing, but it is extremely important that it is triggered prior to the response being constructed and sent back to the server.

OnActionExecutedAsync

> The OnActionExecutedAsync function is identical to the `OnActionExecuted` function with the exception that it works with asynchronous controllers.

Once the `ValidationActionFilterAttribute` is created, it can be implemented globally so that none of the API controllers need to perform the same validation inside of each method.

Global Web API filters are defined in the `WebApiConfig` class that was created in Chapter 8 when we installed Web API. Example 9-3 contains an updated `WebApiConfig` class that registers the `ValidationActionFilterAttribute`.

Example 9-3. Updated WebApiConfig

```
using BootstrapIntroduction.Filters;
using System;
using System.Collections.Generic;
using System.Linq;
using System.Web.Http;

namespace BootstrapIntroduction
{
  public static class WebApiConfig
  {
    public static void Register(HttpConfiguration config)
    {
      // Web API configuration and services
```

```
      config.Filters.Add(new ValidationActionFilterAttribute());

      // Web API routes
      config.MapHttpAttributeRoutes();

      config.Routes.MapHttpRoute(
        name: "DefaultApi",
        routeTemplate: "api/{controller}/{id}",
        defaults: new { id = RouteParameter.Optional }
      );
    }
  }
}
```

Testing the validation is not quite so straightforward. When the authors forms were initially created, they were configured to perform client-side validation to avoid unnecessary requests to the server to perform the same validation.

You can disable this or use a free tool called Fiddler from Telerik to perform a direct request to the authors Web API controller.

Installing Fiddler

You can install Fiddler by visiting Telerik's Fiddler product page (*http://www.telerik.com/fiddler*) and clicking the Free Download button.

Fiddler currently offers an Alpha version for Linux and Mac. Of course, any traffic-monitoring software can be used to perform this test if you prefer not to use Fiddler.

If your web application is not running, be sure it is running now. With Fiddler open, you'll see a handful of tabs near the top right-hand side. In this list is a tab called Composer, which allows you to execute your own web request.

Figure 9-1 contains the setup I used to execute a request to create an author against the REST API previously created.

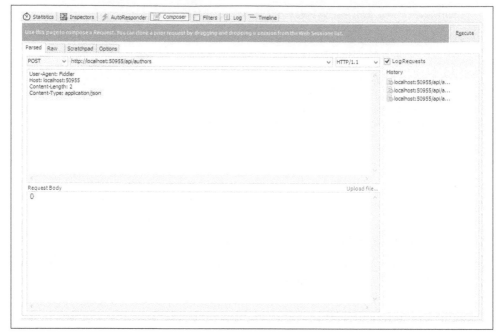

Figure 9-1. Composer settings

There are several key settings required to execute the request:

- A content-type. I used application/json.
- The request type. This must be POST. This is selected from the drop-down beside the URL.
- The URL, it might be slightly different from mine if the random port differs. It's important that you use /api/authors at the end of the URL.
- The request body. I set it to {}, which is JSON syntax for an empty request body.

Finally, you can execute the request by clicking the Execute button near the upper right.

Once your request is executed, it will appear on the left with any other requests that Fiddler is currently monitoring. Find your request and double-click to select it and view the results.

As expected, this request failed with a 400 Bad Request. In Fiddler, you can select the JSON view to see the results returned from the server. Figure 9-2 contains the response from my failed call.

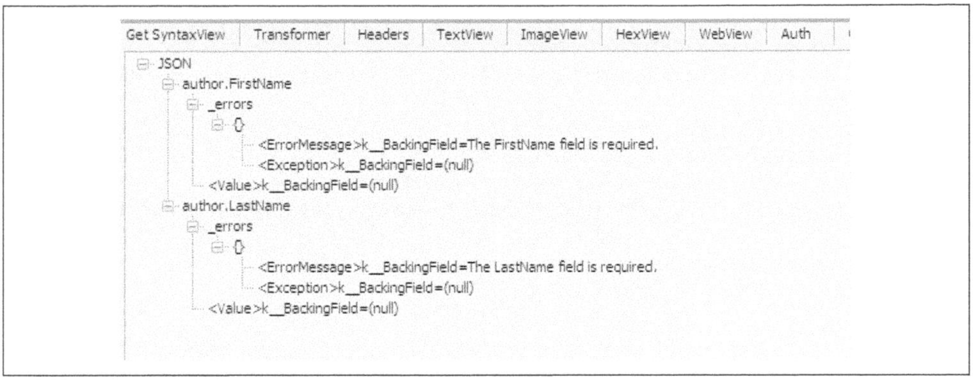

Figure 9-2. 400 Bad Request

Each key in the JSON contains the field that has a validation issue. Inside the field is an array of errors that contains a specific error message that can be used to inform the API integrator why the request is invalid.

Automapping with a Result Filter

In the previous section, the Action filter was added globally to all Web API requests. However, it doesn't make sense to apply all filters globally. Filters can also be added directly to one or more methods in your controller, or if it makes sense, to the entire controller itself.

This section will demonstrate how this is done by creating a custom Result filter. The Result filter will update the `Index` function of the `AuthorsController` to not perform the Automapping and creation of the `ResultList`. The `Index` view will still depend on this; however, as you create more and more controllers with a listing page of the model, the generation of the `ResultList` will quickly become extremely repetitive.

Example 9-4 contains a new class called `GenerateResultListFilterAttribute`, and I have placed it within the previously created *Filters* folder.

Example 9-4. GenerateResultListFilterAttribute

```
using BootstrapIntroduction.Models;
using BootstrapIntroduction.ViewModels;
using System;
using System.Collections.Generic;
using System.ComponentModel;
using System.Linq;
using System.Web;
using System.Web.Mvc;

namespace BootstrapIntroduction.Filters
```

```
{
  [AttributeUsage(AttributeTargets.Method)]
  public class GenerateResultListFilterAttribute : FilterAttribute, IResultFilter
  {
    private readonly Type _sourceType;
    private readonly Type _destinationType;

    public GenerateResultListFilterAttribute(Type sourceType, Type destinationType)
    {
      _sourceType = sourceType;
      _destinationType = destinationType;
    }

    public void OnResultExecuting(ResultExecutingContext filterContext)
    {
      var model = filterContext.Controller.ViewData.Model;

      var resultListGenericType = typeof(ResultList<>)
                  .MakeGenericType(new Type[] { _destinationType });
      var srcGenericType = typeof(List<>).MakeGenericType(
          new Type[] { _sourceType });
      var destGenericType = typeof(List<>).MakeGenericType(
          new Type[] { _destinationType });

      AutoMapper.Mapper.CreateMap(_sourceType, _destinationType);
      var viewModel = AutoMapper.Mapper.Map(model, srcGenericType, destGenericType);

      var queryOptions = filterContext.Controller.ViewData.ContainsKey(
          "QueryOptions") ?
        filterContext.Controller.ViewData["QueryOptions"] :
        new QueryOptions();

      var resultList = Activator.CreateInstance(resultListGenericType, viewModel,
          queryOptions);

      filterContext.Controller.ViewData.Model = resultList;
    }

    public void OnResultExecuted(ResultExecutedContext filterContext)
    {
    }
  }
}
```

This class contains some similarities to the previously created `ValidationActionFil`
`terAttribute` with a few notable differences. The Result filter extends the base `Fil`
`terAttribute` class, and it implements the `IResultFilter` interface.

Implementing the `IResultFilter` requires two functions: `OnResultExecuting` and
`OnResultExecuted`. These functions are quite similar to the Action filter equivalents

in that the first one is called prior to the view being generated, and the second is called after the view is generated and ready to be returned to the server.

This Result filter only implements the OnResultExecuting function because it changes the model that was bound to the View from the Controller to a new Result List model.

The GenerateResultListFilterAttribute expects two input parameters: source Type and destinationType. These two type properties are used to perform the auto-mapping from the data model to the ViewModel. The class is also attributed with an AttributeUsage that indicates this filter can only be used on methods. This is done because of the specific requirements for the constructor.

Inside the OnResultExecuting function, reflection is used to dynamically instantiate the ResultList to the destinationType and populate the results by executing the automapper.

Previously, in the Index function, the QueryOptions were passed to the View in the ViewBag before moving within the ResultList class. This Result filter assumes the QueryOptions will be stored in a similar ViewData dictionary that is accessed via the Result filter and passed to the ResultList class.

A few more changes are required to make this work. Previously, the properties in the ResultList class were being publicly set; this has been updated to accept them via the constructor. Example 9-5 contains an updated ResultList class.

Example 9-5. Updated ResultList

```
using Newtonsoft.Json;
using System;
using System.Collections.Generic;
using System.Linq;
using System.Web;

namespace BootstrapIntroduction.ViewModels
{
  public class ResultList<T>
  {
    public ResultList(List<T> results, QueryOptions queryOptions)
    {
      Results = results;
      QueryOptions = queryOptions;
    }

    [JsonProperty(PropertyName="queryOptions")]
    public QueryOptions QueryOptions { get; private set; }

    [JsonProperty(PropertyName = "results")]
```

```
    public List<T> Results { get; private set; }
  }
}
```

This change will break how the Web API AuthorsController was previously instantiating the ResultList class. Example 9-6 contains an updated Index function to match the change.

Example 9-6. Updated Web API AuthorsController

```
public ResultList<AuthorViewModel> Get([FromUri]QueryOptions queryOptions)
{
  var start = (queryOptions.CurrentPage - 1) * queryOptions.PageSize;

  var authors = db.Authors.
    OrderBy(queryOptions.Sort).
    Skip(start).
    Take(queryOptions.PageSize);

  queryOptions.TotalPages =
    (int)Math.Ceiling((double)db.Authors.Count() / queryOptions.PageSize);

  AutoMapper.Mapper.CreateMap<Author, AuthorViewModel>();

  return new ResultList<AuthorViewModel>(
            AutoMapper.Mapper.Map<List<Author>,
            List<AuthorViewModel>>(authors.ToList()), queryOptions);
}
```

And finally, it's time to update the MVC AuthorsController to leverage the Result filter and remove the now unneeded Automapping code from the Index function. Example 9-7 contains an updated Index function implementing the Result filter.

Example 9-7. Updated MVC AuthorsController

```
[GenerateResultListFilterAttribute(typeof(Author), typeof(AuthorViewModel))]
public ActionResult Index([Form] QueryOptions queryOptions)
{
  var start = (queryOptions.CurrentPage - 1) * queryOptions.PageSize;

  var authors = db.Authors.
    OrderBy(queryOptions.Sort).
    Skip(start).
    Take(queryOptions.PageSize);

  queryOptions.TotalPages =
    (int)Math.Ceiling((double)db.Authors.Count() / queryOptions.PageSize);

  ViewData["QueryOptions"] = queryOptions;
```

```
      return View(authors.ToList());
  }
```

Web API Error Handling

Exceptions happen all the time. Sometimes, it can be an unexpected exception; other times, it is a business validation exception. No matter what type of exception it is, a global Exception filter will help you to deal with all exceptions in a consistent fashion.

Example 9-8 contains a new OnApiExceptionAttribute class. This class can be created in the *Filters* directory. The goal of this class is to build a new HttpResponseMessage with a specific HTTP Status Code based on the type of exception that occurred. The content being returned will also be tailored to suppress unknown server errors.

Example 9-8. OnApiExceptionAttribute

```
using BootstrapIntroduction.ViewModels;
using System;
using System.Collections.Generic;
using System.Linq;
using System.Net;
using System.Net.Http;
using System.Web;
using System.Web.Http.Filters;

namespace BootstrapIntroduction.Filters
{
  public class OnApiExceptionAttribute : ExceptionFilterAttribute
  {
    public override void OnException(HttpActionExecutedContext actionExecutedContext)
    {
      var exceptionType = actionExecutedContext.Exception.GetType().Name;

      ReturnData returnData;

      switch (exceptionType)
      {
        case "ObjectNotFoundException":
          returnData = new ReturnData(HttpStatusCode.NotFound,
            actionExecutedContext.Exception.Message, "Error");
          break;

        default:
          returnData = new ReturnData(HttpStatusCode.InternalServerError,
            "An error occurred, please try again or contact the administrator.",
            "Error");
          break;
      }

      actionExecutedContext.Response =
```

```
      new HttpResponseMessage(returnData.HttpStatusCode)
    {
      Content = new StringContent(returnData.Content),
      ReasonPhrase = returnData.ReasonPhrase
    };
    }
  }
}
```

Creating an Exception filter involves creating a class that inherits from the `Exception FilterAttribute` class. Then you override the `OnException` function and add your custom logic.

Example 9-8 does this, and a `switch` statement is implemented to create a different type of `ReturnData` object (created in Example 9-9) based on the exception that occurred. To start, the switch statement only contains two cases. The first one is when the exception is an `ObjectNotFoundException`, which will return a 404 Not Found exception and set the content of the response to the message within the exception. The second is the default `case` statement, which will return a 500 Internal Server Error. Here the content is set to a generic message to suppress what the actual error was.

As your code expands and you work with new exceptions, this `switch` statement can be extended to return many other different HTTP Status Codes and error content.

The `OnApiExceptionAttribute` leverages a new ViewModel called `ReturnData`. Example 9-9 contains the class definition. This file can be created in the *ViewModels* directory.

Example 9-9. ReturnData ViewModel

```
using System.Net;
namespace BootstrapIntroduction.ViewModels
{
  public class ReturnData
  {
    public ReturnData(HttpStatusCode httpStatusCode, string content,
        string reasonPhrase)
    {
      HttpStatusCode = httpStatusCode;
      Content = content;
      ReasonPhrase = reasonPhrase;
    }

    public HttpStatusCode HttpStatusCode { get; private set; }
    public string Content { get; private set; }
    public string ReasonPhrase { get; private set; }
  }
}
```

Example 9-10 demonstrates how an `ObjectNotFoundException` can be thrown by implementing a new function in the Web API `AuthorsController`.

Example 9-10. Updated Web API AuthorsController

```
// GET: api/Authors/5
[ResponseType(typeof(AuthorViewModel))]
public IHttpActionResult Get(int id)
{
  Author author = db.Authors.Find(id);
  if (author == null)
  {
    throw new System.Data.Entity.Core.ObjectNotFoundException
      (string.Format("Unable to find author with id {0}", id));
  }

  AutoMapper.Mapper.CreateMap<Author, AuthorViewModel>();

  return Ok(AutoMapper.Mapper.Map<Author, AuthorViewModel>(author));
}
```

The final piece of the puzzle is to add your new Exception Attribute to the *WebApi-Config*. Example 9-11 contains an updated *WebApiConfig* that instantiates the new `OnApiExceptionAttribute`.

Example 9-11. Updated WebApiConfig

```
using BootstrapIntroduction.Filters;
using System;
using System.Collections.Generic;
using System.Linq;
using System.Web.Http;

namespace BootstrapIntroduction
{
  public static class WebApiConfig
  {
    public static void Register(HttpConfiguration config)
    {
      // Web API configuration and services
      config.Filters.Add(new ValidationActionFilterAttribute());
      config.Filters.Add(new OnApiExceptionAttribute());

      // Web API routes
      config.MapHttpAttributeRoutes();

      config.Routes.MapHttpRoute(
        name: "DefaultApi",
        routeTemplate: "api/{controller}/{id}",
        defaults: new { id = RouteParameter.Optional }
```

```
          );
      }
    }
}
```

To see this in action, with your web application running, you can navigate to this URL in your web browser: *http://localhost:50955/api/authors/-2*. This will return the error message "Unable to find author with id -2." Please note that your URL might be slightly different if the port 50955 does not match.

MVC Error Handling

Creating an error handler for MVC is quite similar to creating one for Web API. Example 9-12 contains a new OnExceptionAttribute (no "Api" this time) that contains very similar logic to the OnApiExceptionAttribute.

Example 9-12. OnExceptionAttribute

```
using BootstrapIntroduction.ViewModels;
using System;
using System.Net;
using System.Web.Mvc;

namespace BootstrapIntroduction.Filters
{
  public class OnExceptionAttribute : HandleErrorAttribute
  {
    public override void OnException(ExceptionContext exceptionContext)
    {
      var exceptionType = exceptionContext.Exception.GetType().Name;

      ReturnData returnData;

      switch (exceptionType)
      {
        case "ObjectNotFoundException":
          returnData = new ReturnData(HttpStatusCode.NotFound,
            exceptionContext.Exception.Message, "Error");
          break;

        default:
          returnData = new ReturnData(HttpStatusCode.InternalServerError,
            "An error occurred, please try again or contact the administrator.",
            "Error");
          break;
      }

      exceptionContext.Controller.ViewData.Model = returnData.Content;
      exceptionContext.HttpContext.Response.StatusCode =
```

```
      (int)returnData.HttpStatusCode;
    exceptionContext.Result = new ViewResult
    {
      ViewName = "Error",
      ViewData = exceptionContext.Controller.ViewData
    };

    exceptionContext.ExceptionHandled = true;

    base.OnException(exceptionContext);
  }
 }
}
```

The `OnExceptionAttribute` extends the `HandleErrorAttribute`, and it overrides the `OnException` method. The first half of Example 9-12 is an identical `switch` statement that will set up the `ReturnData` object. After this is done, the result that was going to be displayed is altered to return an error view instead.

First, the ViewModel that is bound to a View is updated to write the `Content` from the `ReturnData`. This will be used by the `Error` view shown in Example 9-13. Next, the `StatusCode` of the `Response` is changed (quite similarly to how it was changed in the `OnApiExceptionAttribute`). And finally, a new `ViewResult` is created that will load the *Error.cshtml* view that exists within the *Views/Shared* folder.

After the result has been updated, the exception is marked as handled before calling the base `OnException` function.

Example 9-13 contains an updated *Error.cshtml* view from the *Shared* views folder.

Example 9-13. Updated Error.cshtml

```
@model string
<!DOCTYPE html>
<html>
<head>
  <meta name="viewport" content="width=device-width" />
  <title>Error</title>
</head>
<body>
  <hgroup>
    <h1>Error.</h1>
    <h2>An error occurred while processing your request.</h2>
    <p>@Model</p>
  </hgroup>
</body>
</html>
```

Three minor changes have been made to the default error page. First, a ViewModel of type string has been bound to the view. Second, the Layout = null has been removed, so it will use the shared layout, and the error page will look like the rest of the site. And finally, the ViewModel that is bound to the view is displayed beneath the error headers inside a paragraph tag.

When the `AuthorsController` was first scaffolded, a `Details` function was created that accepts an author ID and will display information about the author. Example 9-14 updates this function to throw an `ObjectNotFoundException` if the author is null (just like Example 9-10 did for the Web API controller).

Example 9-14. Updated MVC AuthorsController

```
// GET: Authors/Details/5
public ActionResult Details(int? id)
{
  if (id == null)
  {
    return new HttpStatusCodeResult(HttpStatusCode.BadRequest);
  }
  Author author = db.Authors.Find(id);
  if (author == null)
  {
    throw new System.Data.Entity.Core.ObjectNotFoundException
      (string.Format("Unable to find author with id {0}", id));
  }

  AutoMapper.Mapper.CreateMap<Author, AuthorViewModel>();
  return View(AutoMapper.Mapper.Map<Author, AuthorViewModel>(author));
}
```

And finally, the `OnExceptionAttribute` needs to be registered in the `FilterConfig` class as shown in Example 9-15.

Example 9-15. Updated FilterConfig

```
using BootstrapIntroduction.Filters;
using System.Web;
using System.Web.Mvc;

namespace BootstrapIntroduction
{
  public class FilterConfig
  {
    public static void RegisterGlobalFilters(GlobalFilterCollection filters)
    {
      filters.Add(new HandleErrorAttribute());
      filters.Add(new OnExceptionAttribute());
```

```
      }
    }
}
```

To see the new error handler in action (as shown in Figure 9-3), you can visit *http://localhost:50955/authors/Details/-2* in your browser.

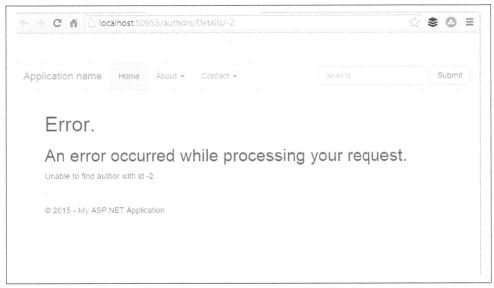

Figure 9-3. Custom error handler

Summary

This chapter demonstrated three of the five different types of global filters you can create. Most of the filters were added globally, but as the Result filter demonstrated, filters can also be applied to individual actions.

MVC also contains many built-in Result and Action filters that you can use. Visit the MSDN description of the FilterAttribute class (*http://bit.ly/action-filter-att*) to see many of the existing Result filters. Likewise, on MSDN you can visit the ActionFilter-Attribute class (*http://bit.ly/act-filter-att*) to see many of the existing Action filter attributes.

CHAPTER 10

Adding Authentication and Authorization

In this chapter, I will demonstrate how to create your own Authentication and Authorization filters. There are many tutorials available on the Internet about setting up FormsAuthentication (*http://bit.ly/formsauth*) together with ASP.NET Membership (*http://bit.ly/asp-members*) to manage users in your application—in fact, this is a built-in option when you create a new MVC application with Visual Studio. To avoid reinventing the wheel, this chapter will implement Basic Access Authentication. Basic authentication allows a web browser to provide a username and password when performing a request against the web server. The authentication is provided in the HTTP Headers as a Base64-encoded string.

Authentication Overview

Authentication filters did not exist prior to MVC 5; instead, it was mixed together in a single Authorization filter. As of MVC 5, there is a nice and clear separation of concerns with authentication and authorization.

Creating a filter involves implementing two functions:

OnAuthentication
> This function is called at the start of the life cycle and is responsible for validating the credentials, if supplied. This is described in more detail in the following text.

OnAuthenticationChallenge
> This function is called at the end of the life cycle for every request. It is responsible for requesting authentication when the request is unauthorized.

The role of the `OnAuthentication` function is three-fold (a flowchart is shown in Figure 10-1):

1. If no authentication is provided, the filter does nothing. This is important because it clearly implies that the Authentication filter doesn't prevent requests because the authentication was not provided. It is left to the Authorization filters to determine whether the user must be authenticated to proceed.
2. If authentication is provided and the credentials are valid, the Authentication filter defines an identity to the application context with an authenticated principal (commonly a user).
3. If authentication is provided and the credentials are invalid, the Authentication filter sets an error result with an unauthorized request. The MVC framework is notified that authentication has failed and should not proceed further.

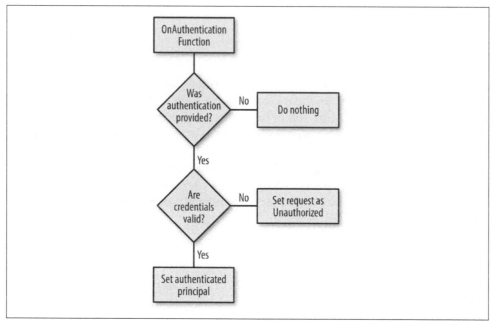

Figure 10-1. OnAuthentication flowchart

Authorization Overview

An Authorization filter no longer needs to validate credentials; instead, it can focus on whether an authenticated principal is set. If the principal is not authenticated, the filter will set the request as unauthorized. Furthermore, an Authorization filter can perform further validation. For example, the default Authorize (*http://bit.ly/auth-att*) attribute can optionally validate that the authenticated principal exists within a specific group, allowing easy role-based authorization.

Figure 10-2 contains a flowchart that demonstrates how the request begins with the Authentication filter and, before returning a response, ends with the Authentication filter.

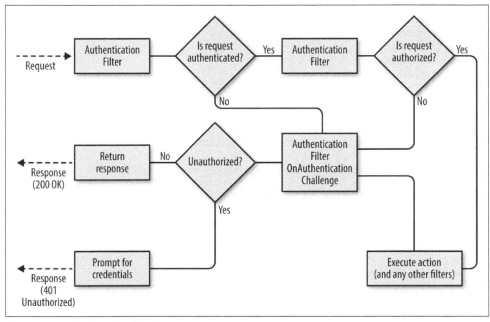

Figure 10-2. Life cycle flowchart

As the flowchart demonstrates, whether the request is successful or unauthenticated/ unauthorized before the response is sent back from the server, the `OnAuthentication Challenge` is called for each request. If the request is not authenticated, it does not proceed on through to authorization. Likewise, if the request is not authorized, it does not proceed with executing the requested action.

Implementing an Authentication Filter

Creating your own Authentication filter involves inheriting from the same `ActionFil terAttribute` used for common Action filters (described in Chapter 9), as well as implementing the `IAuthenticationFilter` interface.

Implementing the `IAuthenticationFilter` interface involves creating the two afore-mentioned functions: `OnAuthentication` and `OnAuthenticationChallenge` (shown in Example 10-1). I've decided to call this class `BasicAuthenticationAttribute` and have created it within the existing *Filters* folder.

Example 10-1. Empty Authentication filter

```
using BootstrapIntroduction.Models;
using System;
using System.Linq;
using System.Net;
using System.Security.Principal;
using System.Text;
using System.Web.Mvc;
using System.Web.Mvc.Filters;

namespace BootstrapIntroduction.Filters
{
  public class BasicAuthenticationAttribute
      : ActionFilterAttribute, IAuthenticationFilter
  {
    public void OnAuthentication(AuthenticationContext filterContext)
    {
    }

    public void OnAuthenticationChallenge(AuthenticationChallengeContext
        filterContext)
    {
    }
  }
}
```

The first thing the `OnAuthentication` function will do is check whether the `Authori` `zation` header is set in the `filterContext` request headers. If no authorization is found, or it doesn't contain the word "Basic" in it, the function returns and stops processing (shown in Example 10-2).

Example 10-2. Checking for authorization

```
using BootstrapIntroduction.Models;
using System;
using System.Linq;
using System.Net;
using System.Security.Principal;
using System.Text;
using System.Web.Mvc;
using System.Web.Mvc.Filters;

namespace BootstrapIntroduction.Filters
{
  public class BasicAuthenticationAttribute
      : ActionFilterAttribute, IAuthenticationFilter
  {
    public void OnAuthentication(AuthenticationContext filterContext)
    {
      var request = filterContext.HttpContext.Request;
```

```
      var authorization = request.Headers["Authorization"];

      // No authorization, do nothing
      if (string.IsNullOrEmpty(authorization) || !authorization.Contains("Basic"))
        return;
    }

    public void OnAuthenticationChallenge(AuthenticationChallengeContext
        filterContext)
    {
    }
  }
}
```

If the authorization is found in the request header, the function proceeds to parse out the username and password from the header. The authorization is Base64 encoded, so the first thing to do is Base64 decode the string. At this time, it is also removing the word "Basic" to focus on extracting the username and password. The decoded string is stored in a byte array, so this is extracted into a usable string. And finally, with that string, the username and password are separated by a colon (:), so the string is split up by this value and stores the username and password into local variables for further use. This is shown in Example 10-3.

Example 10-3. Extracting the username and password

```
using BootstrapIntroduction.Models;
using System;
using System.Linq;
using System.Net;
using System.Security.Principal;
using System.Text;
using System.Web.Mvc;
using System.Web.Mvc.Filters;

namespace BootstrapIntroduction.Filters
{
  public class BasicAuthenticationAttribute
      : ActionFilterAttribute, IAuthenticationFilter
  {
    public void OnAuthentication(AuthenticationContext filterContext)
    {
      var request = filterContext.HttpContext.Request;
      var authorization = request.Headers["Authorization"];

      // No authorization, do nothing
      if (string.IsNullOrEmpty(authorization) || !authorization.Contains("Basic"))
        return;

      // Parse username and password from header
      byte[] encodedDataAsBytes = Convert.FromBase64String(
```

```
      authorization.Replace("Basic ", ""));
    string value = Encoding.ASCII.GetString(encodedDataAsBytes);

    string username = value.Substring(0, value.IndexOf(':'));
    string password = value.Substring(value.IndexOf(':') + 1);
  }

  public void OnAuthenticationChallenge(AuthenticationChallengeContext
      filterContext)
  {
  }
 }
}
```

Now it's time for the validation. Two different validation checks are performed. First, I think it's a good idea to ensure that both the username and password are not empty strings. If either are, the result is set to an HttpUnauthorizedResult.

Once we know the username and password are properly set, they are used to find a valid user of the system. In this example, I've created a new User model (shown in Example 10-7) and an AuthenticatedUsers list (shown in Example 10-8) that contains a list of valid usernames and passwords. This list is searched for a matching username and password combination. If no user is found, the result is set to an HttpU nauthorizedResult. If a user is found, a new GenericPrincipal is instantiated with the user that matched the criteria. This is shown in Example 10-4.

Example 10-4. Authenticating the user

```
using BootstrapIntroduction.Models;
using System;
using System.Linq;
using System.Net;
using System.Security.Principal;
using System.Text;
using System.Web.Mvc;
using System.Web.Mvc.Filters;

namespace BootstrapIntroduction.Filters
{
  public class BasicAuthenticationAttribute
      : ActionFilterAttribute, IAuthenticationFilter
  {
    public void OnAuthentication(AuthenticationContext filterContext)
    {
      var request = filterContext.HttpContext.Request;
      var authorization = request.Headers["Authorization"];

      // No authorization, do nothing
      if (string.IsNullOrEmpty(authorization) || !authorization.Contains("Basic"))
        return;
```

```
    // Parse username and password from header
    byte[] encodedDataAsBytes = Convert.FromBase64String(
        authorization.Replace("Basic ", ""));
    string value = Encoding.ASCII.GetString(encodedDataAsBytes);

    string username = value.Substring(0, value.IndexOf(':'));
    string password = value.Substring(value.IndexOf(':') + 1);

    if (string.IsNullOrEmpty(username) || string.IsNullOrEmpty(password))
    {
      filterContext.Result = new HttpUnauthorizedResult(
          "Username or password missing");
      return;
    }

    // Validate username and password
    var user = AuthenticatedUsers.Users
                .FirstOrDefault(u => u.Name == username && u.Password
                    == password);

    if (user == null)
    {
      filterContext.Result = new HttpUnauthorizedResult(
          "Invalid username and password");
      return;
    }

    // Set principal
    filterContext.Principal = new GenericPrincipal(user, user.Roles);
  }

  public void OnAuthenticationChallenge(AuthenticationChallengeContext
      filterContext)
  {
  }
 }
}
```

And finally, to complete the Authentication filter, the OnAuthenticationChallenge that executes every time will generate a new result that encapsulates the current result (more on this in a minute). Once the request is executed, it can assert that the Status Code is not set to 401 Unauthorized. If it is an unauthorized request, it adds a WWW-Authenticate header with the value of Basic. When a browser receives this header, it will prompt the user for credentials as shown in Figure 10-3. Example 10-5 demonstrates the OnAuthenticationChallenge function.

Example 10-5. OnAuthenticationChallenge

```
using BootstrapIntroduction.Models;
using System;
using System.Linq;
using System.Net;
using System.Security.Principal;
using System.Text;
using System.Web.Mvc;
using System.Web.Mvc.Filters;

namespace BootstrapIntroduction.Filters
{
  public class BasicAuthenticationAttribute
      : ActionFilterAttribute, IAuthenticationFilter
  {
    public void OnAuthentication(AuthenticationContext filterContext)
    {
            // Truncated for example
    }

    public void OnAuthenticationChallenge(AuthenticationChallengeContext
        filterContext)
    {
      filterContext.Result = new BasicChallengeActionResult
      {
        CurrrentResult = filterContext.Result
      };
    }
  }
}
```

Example 10-5 sets the result to a newly generated `BasicChallengeActionResult` (shown in Example 10-6). This class extends the basic `ActionResult` and contains a public property called `CurrentResult`. The `OnAuthenticationChallenge` function instantiates this class and sets the `CurrentResult` with the current `filterCon text.Result`. Example 10-6 overrides the `ExecuteResult` function, and the first thing it does is execute the `CurrentResult`. Doing this will allow the next step to happen, which is to determine if the response is 401 unauthorized. If it is, the `WWW-Authenticate` header is added.

Example 10-6. BasicChallengeActionResult

```
using BootstrapIntroduction.Models;
using System;
using System.Linq;
using System.Net;
using System.Security.Principal;
using System.Text;
using System.Web.Mvc;
```

```csharp
using System.Web.Mvc.Filters;

namespace BootstrapIntroduction.Filters
{
  public class BasicAuthenticationAttribute : ActionFilterAttribute,
      IAuthenticationFilter
  {
    public void OnAuthentication(AuthenticationContext filterContext)
    {
        // Truncated for example
    }

    public void OnAuthenticationChallenge(AuthenticationChallengeContext
        filterContext)
    {
      filterContext.Result = new BasicChallengeActionResult
      {
        CurrrentResult = filterContext.Result
      };
    }
  }

  class BasicChallengeActionResult : ActionResult
  {
    public ActionResult CurrrentResult { get; set; }

    public override void ExecuteResult(ControllerContext context)
    {
      CurrrentResult.ExecuteResult(context);

      var response = context.HttpContext.Response;

      if (response.StatusCode == (int)HttpStatusCode.Unauthorized)
        response.AddHeader("WWW-Authenticate", "Basic");
    }
  }
}
```

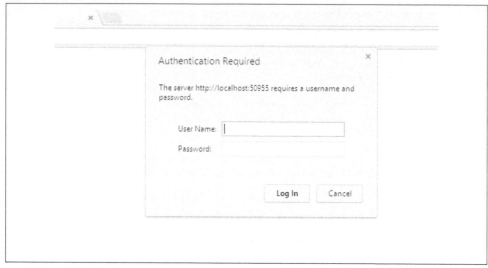

Figure 10-3. Basic authentication

Before this example will compile, the `User` model class and `AuthenticatedUsers` class need to be created. Example 10-7 creates a new class in the *Models* directory called `User`.

Example 10-7. User Model

```
using System.Collections.Generic;
using System.Security.Principal;

namespace BootstrapIntroduction.Models
{
  public class User : IIdentity
  {
    public User(string username, string password, string[] roles,
        List<string> validIpAddresses)
    {
      Name = username;
      Password = password;
      Roles = roles;
      ValidIpAddresses = validIpAddresses;
    }

    public string Name { get; private set; }

    public string Password { get; private set; }

    public string[] Roles { get; private set; }

    public List<string> ValidIpAddresses { get; private set; }
```

```
    public bool IsAuthenticated { get { return true; } }

    public string AuthenticationType { get { return "Basic"; } }
  }
}
```

The User model implements the IIdentity interface, which requires three properties to be set: AuthenticationType, IsAuthenticated, and Name. Because the model implements the IIdentity interface, as demonstrated in Example 10-4, the User can be set when the new GenericPrincipal is instantiated.

The User model also contains properties for a list of Roles and a list of ValidIpAd dresses and, of course, a password. The username is stored in the required Name property. The list of ValidIpAddresses will be used in the next section when a custom Authorization filter is created.

And finally, a new AuthenticatedUsers class can be created in the same *Models* folder. Example 10-8 shows the AuthenticatedUsers class.

Example 10-8. AuthenticatedUsers

```
using System.Collections.Generic;
namespace BootstrapIntroduction.Models
{
  public static class AuthenticatedUsers
  {
    private static List<User> _users = new List<User>
    {
      new User("jamie", "munro", null, new List<string> { "::1" } )
    };

    public static List<User> Users { get { return _users; } }
  }
}
```

The AuthenticatedUsers class contains a public list of Users that are used in Example 10-4 to search this list for a user that contains the same username and password. The AuthenticatedUsers is a static class that, during application start, creates a list of valid users. In this scenario, I have created one user with a username of jamie and a password of munro. The roles are set to null because they are currently not required for this example. ValidIpAddresses is instantiated with a single item that contains the value ::1 (more on this in the next section).

Implementing the Authentication filter can be done in one of two ways: globally or on a per-controller/action basis. Because the Authentication filter is only responsible for validating authorization credentials, if they are provided, I think it makes most sense to apply this globally. However, when it comes to authorization, I think it makes more sense to apply on a per-controller/action basis (unless your entire site requires authorization).

Example 10-9 updates the FilterConfig class inside the *App_Start* directory to register the new BasicAuthenticationAttribute across all requests.

Example 10-9. BasicAuthentication globally

```
using BootstrapIntroduction.Filters;
using System.Web;
using System.Web.Mvc;

namespace BootstrapIntroduction
{
  public class FilterConfig
  {
    public static void RegisterGlobalFilters(GlobalFilterCollection filters)
    {
      filters.Add(new HandleErrorAttribute());
      filters.Add(new OnExceptionAttribute());
      filters.Add(new BasicAuthenticationAttribute());
    }
  }
}
```

Implementing an Authorization Filter

Creating your own Authorization filter involves creating a class that extends the existing AuthorizeAttribute and overriding the OnAuthorization function. Example 10-10 creates a new BasicAuthorizationAttribute class inside the existing *Filters* folder.

Example 10-10. Empty BasicAuthorizationAttribute

```
using BootstrapIntroduction.Models;
using System.Web.Mvc;

namespace BootstrapIntroduction.Filters
{
  public class BasicAuthorizationAttribute : AuthorizeAttribute
  {
    public override void OnAuthorization(AuthorizationContext filterContext)
    {
    }
  }
}
```

The first responsibility of the OnAuthorization function is to check that there is a valid User. Example 10-11 demonstrates this, and if there is no user or the user is not authenticated, the result is set to HttpUnauthorizedResult and processing stops.

Example 10-11. Checking for valid user

```
using BootstrapIntroduction.Models;
using System.Web.Mvc;

namespace BootstrapIntroduction.Filters
{
  public class BasicAuthorizationAttribute : AuthorizeAttribute
  {
    public override void OnAuthorization(AuthorizationContext filterContext)
    {
      var userIdentity = filterContext.HttpContext.User.Identity as User;

      if (userIdentity == null || !userIdentity.IsAuthenticated)
      {
        filterContext.Result = new HttpUnauthorizedResult();
        return;
      }
    }
  }
}
```

So far, the Authorization filter does nothing custom. If you recall back in the previous section, when the User model was created, it contained a list of validIpAddresses. Let's put those to good use. Example 10-12 extracts the user's IP address from the server variables. The IP address can be set in one of three spots, depending on things like if the user is using a proxy, browsing from localhost (like I am), etc.

Example 10-12. Extracting the IP address

```
using BootstrapIntroduction.Models;
using System.Web.Mvc;

namespace BootstrapIntroduction.Filters
{
  public class BasicAuthorizationAttribute : AuthorizeAttribute
  {
    public override void OnAuthorization(AuthorizationContext filterContext)
    {
      var userIdentity = filterContext.HttpContext.User.Identity as User;

      if (userIdentity == null || !userIdentity.IsAuthenticated)
      {
        filterContext.Result = new HttpUnauthorizedResult();
        return;
```

```
      }

      string visitorIPAddress =
        filterContext.HttpContext.Request.ServerVariables["HTTP_X_FORWARDED_FOR"];

      if (string.IsNullOrEmpty(visitorIPAddress)) visitorIPAddress =
        filterContext.HttpContext.Request.ServerVariables["REMOTE_ADDR"];

      if (string.IsNullOrEmpty(visitorIPAddress))
        visitorIPAddress = filterContext.HttpContext.Request.UserHostAddress;
    }
  }
}
```

With the user's IP address, the custom authorization will validate that the IP address exists within the logged-in User list of ValidIpAddresses. As shown in Example 10-13, if the IP address is not in the list, the request is set to HttpUnauthorizedRe sult; otherwise, the authorization has succeeded, and MVC continues executing down the chain to the action requested.

Example 10-13. Validating the IP address

```
using BootstrapIntroduction.Models;
using System.Web.Mvc;

namespace BootstrapIntroduction.Filters
{
  public class BasicAuthorizationAttribute : AuthorizeAttribute
  {
    public override void OnAuthorization(AuthorizationContext filterContext)
    {
      var userIdentity = filterContext.HttpContext.User.Identity as User;

      if (userIdentity == null || !userIdentity.IsAuthenticated)
      {
        filterContext.Result = new HttpUnauthorizedResult();
        return;
      }

      string visitorIPAddress =
        filterContext.HttpContext.Request.ServerVariables["HTTP_X_FORWARDED_FOR"];

      if (string.IsNullOrEmpty(visitorIPAddress)) visitorIPAddress =
        filterContext.HttpContext.Request.ServerVariables["REMOTE_ADDR"];

      if (string.IsNullOrEmpty(visitorIPAddress))
        visitorIPAddress = filterContext.HttpContext.Request.UserHostAddress;

      if (userIdentity.ValidIpAddresses != null &&
                !userIdentity.ValidIpAddresses.Contains(visitorIPAddress))
```

```
      {
        filterContext.Result = new HttpUnauthorizedResult();
        return;
      }
    }
  }
}
```

Like all filters, the `BasicAuthorizationAttribute` can be implemented globally or on a per-controller/action level. Based on the current site's functionality, I would implement it only on the actions that require security. For example, most of the site is public; however, I might only want authenticated users to be able to add, edit, and delete authors. Example 10-14 contains an abbreviated `AuthorsController` that enforces authorization on the aforementioned actions.

Example 10-14. Adding authorization to AuthorsController

```
using System;
using System.Collections.Generic;
using System.Data;
using System.Data.Entity;
using System.Linq;
namespace BootstrapIntroduction.Controllers
{
  public class AuthorsController : Controller
  {
      // Truncated for example

    // GET: Authors/Create
    [BasicAuthorization]
    public ActionResult Create()
    {
      return View("Form", new AuthorViewModel());
    }

    // GET: Authors/Edit/5
    [BasicAuthorization]
    public ActionResult Edit(int? id)
    {
        // Truncated for example
    }

    // GET: Authors/Delete/5
    [BasicAuthorization]
    public ActionResult Delete(int? id)
    {
        // Truncated for example
    }

    // POST: Authors/Delete/5
```

```
    [HttpPost, ActionName("Delete")]
    [ValidateAntiForgeryToken]
    [BasicAuthorization]
    public ActionResult DeleteConfirmed(int id)
    {
            // Truncated for example
    }
  }
}
```

If you debug your web application and attempt to add a new author, you would receive a request for authentication as shown earlier in Figure 10-3.

Summary

This chapter has demonstrated how to create your own custom Authentication and Authorization filters. To make the examples more focused on the inner workings of these filters, proper security of passwords and storage of user data in a database was not demonstrated. I would encourage that your next steps be to create a new MVC application from Visual Studio and select one of the built-in authorization methods.

The new project will provide a ton of code to implement FormsAuthentication (*http://bit.ly/formsauth*) together with ASP.NET Membership (*http://bit.ly/asp-members*). The ASP.NET Membership provides great functionality for managing your users in a database with password hashing and many other security features. As a great exercise, after you review how it works, try replacing the static `Authenticate dUsers` class with the ASP.NET Membership in the `BasicAuthenticationAttribute`.

CHAPTER 11

URL Routing Using Attributes

In Chapter 1, I reviewed the default route that allows new controllers and new actions to be created and automatically routed based on their names alone. This is extremely convenient and works most of the time. However, whether it is for Search Engine Optimization (SEO) purposes or to follow a naming convention and provide a more convenient URL, custom routing allows you to do this.

Prior to MVC 5, routes were defined in the *RouteConfig* (for MVC) and *WebApiConfig* (for Web Api) and still can be (as the default route is defined). New in MVC 5 is the ability to route via attributes.

Attribute routing is extremely convenient because it helps unhide the routing and makes it more obvious to the developer how the controller and action can be accessed. Global routing, of course, still serves a useful purpose when you have one or two common routes that apply across multiple controllers and/or actions.

Attribute Routing Basics

Before attribute routing can be used, it must be turned on. This is done in the `Route Config` class inside the *App_Start* folder. Example 11-1 contains an updated defintion of this class.

Example 11-1. Updated RouteConfig

```
using System;
using System.Collections.Generic;
using System.Linq;
using System.Web;
using System.Web.Mvc;
using System.Web.Routing;
```

```
namespace BootstrapIntroduction
{
  public class RouteConfig
  {
    public static void RegisterRoutes(RouteCollection routes)
    {
      routes.IgnoreRoute("{resource}.axd/{*pathInfo}");

      routes.MapMvcAttributeRoutes();

      routes.MapRoute(
        name: "Default",
        url: "{controller}/{action}/{id}",
        defaults: new { controller = "Home", action = "Index"
            , id = UrlParameter.Optional }
      );
    }
  }
}
```

Defining a route consists of adding a relative URL from the domain inside of an attribute named Route. A very common scenario where I use routing is for static pages. When the project was first created, a HomeController was created with three actions: Index, About, and Contact. For SEO purposes, it might make more sense for the contact and about pages to reside simply at */About* or */Contact* instead of */Home/ About* and */Home/Contact*, respectively.

This, of course, could be accomplished by making new controllers called AboutCon troller and ContactController, each with a single action called Index. Although this works, it feels a bit like overkill to create new controllers for static pages with a single action.

Enter routing. Example 11-2 contains an updated HomeController with attribute routes for both the About and Contact actions that remove the requirement for the */Home prefix*.

Example 11-2. Updated HomeController

```
using BootstrapIntroduction.Filters;
using BootstrapIntroduction.ViewModels;
using System;
using System.Collections.Generic;
using System.Linq;
using System.Web;
using System.Web.Mvc;

namespace BootstrapIntroduction.Controllers
{
  public class HomeController : Controller
```

```
  {
    public ActionResult Index()
    {
      return View();
    }

    [Route("About")]
    public ActionResult About()
    {
      ViewBag.Message = "Your application description page.";

      return View();
    }

    [Route("Contact")]
    public ActionResult Contact()
    {
      ViewBag.Message = "Your contact page.";

      return View();
    }
  }
}
```

This is one of the most basic examples. Routes can be more complicated. They can define input parameters for your actions, including optional parameters. If you attempted to apply the lessons learned from Part II from the AuthorsController to the BooksController, you may have already created it. If not, you can add the Book sController to the *Controllers* folder now. Example 11-3 contains a new action in a BooksController with a custom attribute. The action is called ByAuthor and accepts an integer called authorId. Because of the default route, this could be accessed via */Books/ByAuthor/{id}*. This example overrides this route and makes the URL look a bit nicer by changing it to */Authors/{id}/Books*.

Example 11-3. BooksController

```
using System;
using System.Collections.Generic;
using System.Data;
using System.Data.Entity;
using System.Linq;
using System.Net;
using System.Web;
using System.Web.Mvc;
using BootstrapIntroduction.DAL;
using BootstrapIntroduction.Models;

namespace BootstrapIntroduction.Controllers
{
```

```
public class BooksController : Controller
{
  private BookContext db = new BookContext();

  [Route("authors/{id}/books")]
  public ActionResult ByAuthor(int id)
  {
    var books = db.Books.Where(b => b.AuthorId == id);
    return View(books.ToList());
  }
}
}
```

You might be asking yourself why this is placed in the `BooksController` and not the `AuthorsController`. My reasoning behind it is about the resources being displayed, which are books, even though the filter is by author. Likewise, if you were viewing the details of a book and wanted more information on the author, a similar route could be inversed. It would exist in the `AuthorsController` and be */Books/{id}/Author*. Because in this case the resource is the author, and it belongs in the `AuthorsControl ler`, even though the filter is by book.

In certain scenarios you may wish to make your input parameters optional. This is accomplished by placing a question mark (?) at the end of the parameter name but inside the closing bracket (as shown in Example 11-4).

Example 11-4. Example optional route

```
[Route("Details/{id?}")]
```

One final common thing done with attribute routing is to define an alternative default route for the controller. The default route will display the `Index` method when no action is defined in the URL. With attribute routing, the default route can be updated by placing the `Route` attribute before the `Controller` definition as shown in Example 11-5.

Example 11-5. Default controller route

```
using BootstrapIntroduction.Filters;
using BootstrapIntroduction.ViewModels;
using System;
using System.Collections.Generic;
using System.Linq;
using System.Web;
using System.Web.Mvc;

namespace BootstrapIntroduction.Controllers
{
  [Route("{action=About}")]
```

```
public class HomeController : Controller
{
    // Truncated for example
}
}
```

This example demonstrates this by updating the HomeController and making the default action the About method.

Route Prefixes

A route prefix allows you to define a common prefix for all actions in your controller. This is quite common when you wish to name your controller to match a pluralized model name, but for SEO (or even readability) purposes, replace it with a different name.

As an example, a synonym for "author" is "writer." Perhaps to visitors of our website, this is a more commonly understood term. Example 11-6 adds a route prefix to the AuthorsController, changing the previous URLs from *Authors* to *Writer*.

Example 11-6. Prefix on AuthorsController

```
using System;
using System.Collections.Generic;
using System.Net;
using System.Web;
using System.Web.ModelBinding;
using System.Web.Mvc;
using BootstrapIntroduction.Models;
using BootstrapIntroduction.ViewModels;
using BootstrapIntroduction.Filters;
using BootstrapIntroduction.Services;

namespace BootstrapIntroduction.Controllers
{
  [RoutePrefix("Writer")]
  public class AuthorsController : Controller
  {
      // Truncated for example
  }
}
```

Having a nonpluralized URL works great for actions that include an id parameter at the end, e.g., */writer/details/{id}*. However, it doesn't make a lot of sense when you are going to the Index action and getting a list of writers. Example 11-7 overrides the route prefix for the Index action only of the AuthorsController.

Example 11-7. Updated Index action

```
[GenerateResultListFilterAttribute(typeof(Author), typeof(AuthorViewModel))]
[Route("~/Writers")]
public ActionResult Index([Form] QueryOptions queryOptions)
{
    var authors = authorService.Get(queryOptions);

    ViewData["QueryOptions"] = queryOptions;

    return View(authors);
}
```

Overriding the route prefix is accomplished by defining a route and placing a tilde (~) followed by a forward slash (/). If the ~/ was not added, the term *writers* would be added to the route prefix making the URL */writer/writers*.

Routing Constraints

This is my favorite enhancement to routing with MVC 5. Prior to MVC 5, routing constraints required regular expressions. With attribute routing, it has become as simple as specifying a constraint type preceded by a colon (:) after the variable name.

Example 11-8 updates the Details action in the AuthorsController to constrain the id to be an integer.

Example 11-8. Updated AuthorsController

```
[Route("Details/{id:int?}")]
public ActionResult Details(int? id)
{
    if (id == null)
    {
        return new HttpStatusCodeResult(HttpStatusCode.BadRequest);
    }

    var author = authorService.GetById(id.Value);

    return View(AutoMapper.Mapper.Map<Author, AuthorViewModel>(author));
}
```

The question mark (?) to mark the id as optional should always be added at the end of the constraints. Notice how I pluralized constraints because they can be chained together. Example 11-9 further updates the Details route to force a minimum value of 0.

Example 11-9. Chaining constraints

```
[Route("Details/{id:int:min(0)?}")]
public ActionResult Details(int? id)
{
  if (id == null)
  {
    return new HttpStatusCodeResult(HttpStatusCode.BadRequest);
  }

  var author = authorService.GetById(id.Value);

  return View(AutoMapper.Mapper.Map<Author, AuthorViewModel>(author));
}
```

Certain constraints (such as the `min` constraint) require input parameters to it, which are done by placing the value within brackets after the constraint.

Chaining the constraints is accomplished by adding a colon (:) before the next constraint.

A complete list of supported constraints is shown in Figure 11-1.

Constraint	Description	Example
alpha	Matches uppercase or lowercase Latin alphabet characters (a-z, A-Z)	{x:alpha}
bool	Matches a Boolean value.	{x:bool}
datetime	Matches a **DateTime** value.	{x:datetime}
decimal	Matches a decimal value.	{x:decimal}
double	Matches a 64-bit floating-point value.	{x:double}
float	Matches a 32-bit floating-point value.	{x:float}
guid	Matches a GUID value.	{x:guid}
int	Matches a 32-bit integer value.	{x:int}
length	Matches a string with the specified length or within a specified range of lengths.	{x:length(6)} {x:length(1,20)}
long	Matches a 64-bit integer value.	{x:long}
max	Matches an integer with a maximum value.	{x:max(10)}
maxlength	Matches a string with a maximum length.	{x:maxlength(10)}
min	Matches an integer with a minimum value.	{x:min(10)}
minlength	Matches a string with a minimum length.	{x:minlength(10)}
range	Matches an integer within a range of values.	{x:range(10,50)}
regex	Matches a regular expression.	{x:regex(^\d{3}-\d{3}-\d{4}$)}

Figure 11-1. Support constraints. This list is courtesy of the MSDN blog (http://bit.ly/att-route)

To complete this section, here is a great way I use routing attributes to make both the URLs and Controllers nice and clean. It's quite common for SEO purposes not to use integers when viewing the details of things like authors or books. Example 11-10 adds two new functions to the AuthorsController (replacing the previous Details method) to display the author either by id or by name.

Example 11-10. Updated AuthorsController

```
// GET: Authors/Details/5
[Route("Details/{id:int:min(0)?}")]
public ActionResult GetById(int? id)
{
  if (id == null)
  {
    return new HttpStatusCodeResult(HttpStatusCode.BadRequest);
  }

  var author = authorService.GetById(id.Value);

  return View(AutoMapper.Mapper.Map<Author, AuthorViewModel>(author));
}

// GET: Authors/Details/Jamie Munro
[Route("Details/{name}")]
public ActionResult GetByName(string name)
{
  if (string.IsNullOrEmpty(name))
  {
    return new HttpStatusCodeResult(HttpStatusCode.BadRequest);
  }

  var author = authorService.GetByName(name);

  return View(AutoMapper.Mapper.Map<Author, AuthorViewModel>(author));
}
```

Both the GetById and GetByName functions route to *Writer/Details*, and because of the constraints, MVC will determine which function to call by parsing out the parameter after Details in the URL. If it is determined to be an integer, it will call the Get ById function. Otherwise, it will call the GetByName function.

For this example to compile, the AuthorService needs to be updated to add the new GetByName method, as is shown in Example 11-11.

Example 11-11. Updated AuthorService

```
using BootstrapIntroduction.Behaviors;
using BootstrapIntroduction.DAL;
using BootstrapIntroduction.Models;
```

```csharp
using BootstrapIntroduction.ViewModels;
using System;
using System.Collections.Generic;
using System.Data.Entity;
using System.Linq;
using System.Linq.Dynamic;
using System.Net;
using System.Web;
using System.Web.Mvc;

namespace BootstrapIntroduction.Services
{
  public class AuthorService : IDisposable
  {
    private BookContext db = new BookContext();

    public List<Author> Get(QueryOptions queryOptions)
    {
      var start = QueryOptionsCalculator.CalculateStart(queryOptions);

      var authors = db.Authors.
        OrderBy(queryOptions.Sort).
        Skip(start).
        Take(queryOptions.PageSize);

      queryOptions.TotalPages = QueryOptionsCalculator.CaclulateTotalPages(
        db.Authors.Count(), queryOptions.PageSize);

      return authors.ToList();
    }

    public Author GetById(long id)
    {
      Author author = db.Authors.Find(id);
      if (author == null)
      {
        throw new System.Data.Entity.Core.ObjectNotFoundException
          (string.Format("Unable to find author with id {0}", id));
      }

      return author;
    }

    public Author GetByName(string name)
    {
      Author author = db.Authors
        .Where(a => a.FirstName + ' ' + a.LastName == name)
        .SingleOrDefault();
      if (author == null)
      {
        throw new System.Data.Entity.Core.ObjectNotFoundException
          (string.Format("Unable to find author with name {0}", name));
```

```
    }

    return author;
  }

  public void Insert(Author author)
  {
    db.Authors.Add(author);

    db.SaveChanges();
  }

  public void Update(Author author)
  {
    db.Entry(author).State = EntityState.Modified;

    db.SaveChanges();
  }

  public void Delete(Author author)
  {
    db.Authors.Remove(author);

    db.SaveChanges();
  }

  public void Dispose() {
    db.Dispose();
  }
  }
}
```

With the addition of these two new functions, authors can be found in one of two ways:

- /Writer/Details/1
- /Writer/Details/Jamie Munro

Summary

Attribute routing is new to MVC 5, which provides a lot of power for creating intelligent routing with a simple mechanism for constraining the data input. It's nice to have the routing inline with the controllers because it can be difficult to understand why a controller method cannot be found when the routing is at a more global level. With attribute routing, the route is defined in the same code as the controller method that you are working on.

CHAPTER 12

Fat Model, Skinny Controller

Up to this point, the examples in this book have been applying the opposite of a fat model, skinny controller, which is a fat controller, skinny model. The term "fat" implies the presence of business logic; "skinny" implies the lack thereof. This was done to provide focus on the new features that were being shown. In fact, you may have noticed in Chapter 8 when Web API was introduced that the MVC and Web API `AuthorsController` contained duplicated code to fetch the list of authors.

That is a perfect example of why fat controllers are convoluted, hard to maintain, and share code between them, whereas the fat model is completely geared toward reusability of code within your application.

Implementing the fat model can be done many different ways, and the depth of organization within can be from one to many layers. This all depends on the complexity of your application.

No matter which approach you take, the end goal of the fat model is to place all of your business logic in the M of MVC. The M should be able to stand alone as a complete application (without a user interface). The V and C that interact to make it MVC can be a console application, a RESTful API, a web application, etc. It shouldn't matter to the M.

This chapter will provide an overview of common ways to separate the concerns within your MVC application followed by an example of refactoring the two `Author sControllers` to share common business logic.

Separation of Concerns

This section will discuss common ways to separate your code within an MVC application. In this section, I will discuss layers upon layers that, depending on the size of your application, may or may not be needed. The next section will demonstrate a subset of these layers that provides a clear separation of concerns. The nice part is that as your application grows and the additional layers are required, you'll have clear spots in which to add them to make your application more organized and easier to maintain.

Controllers

When I build a controller, I think it should perform the following roles:

Data Sanitation/Validation
> A controller receives a request that often contains data, whether it is from a form or the URL. This data needs to be sanitized and validated. This is demonstrated throughout this book where the controller is checking that the `ModelState` is valid. However, the controller is not responsible for performing business validation. It doesn't need to know. It simply should make sure an email is an email or a first name is populated, etc.

Convert Data for the Fat Model
> Chapter 7 introduced server-side ViewModels. The actions that accepted data (`Create` and `Edit`) were updated to accept ViewModels. The fat model speaks only in data models and does not even know that ViewModels exist. It is the controller's job to accept ViewModels from the request and convert them to data models for the business layer to execute on.

Convert Data for the View
> The controller requests data from the fat model and then converts this to a ViewModel before binding the data to the View. Just like the fat model doesn't speak in ViewModels, the View doesn't speak in data models.

Services

I like to think of services as the middleman between controllers and the business logic. A controller calls a service to fetch data, save data, apply the business logic, etc.

This is where the layers can really start to grow, depending on the size of your application. A first stage refactoring that would provide a lot of reusability would be to move the access of the `BookContext` from the `AuthorsController` into an `AuthorService`. This is demonstrated in the next section.

It might be immediately evident that services are responsible for a lot of different things. This is where even more layers can be added beneath (and above) the services layer to further seperate these concerns.

Behaviors

The idea of the behavior layer is to perform as much logic as possible, whether it is simple math, complex business validation, manipulation of data, or other types of logic.

Behaviors accept models and often manipulate or validate them. If a behavior requires data, it should be provided.

By limiting the number of dependencies to your behavior, it can be extremely easy to test. By placing all (or as much as humanly possible) logic within behaviors, the complex business logic is both easy to reuse and easy to test. Both are very important factors for making your application easy to mainain.

The next section will demonstrate how behaviors are called by the service layer to perform business logic.

Repositories

The purpose of the repository layer is two-fold. The first is to place common queries that are used by multiple services in a reusable spot. The second is to remove the database framework dependency in the service layer. This allows the service layer to not concern itself with how to access the data, but just request the data it requires.

Ideally, the only thing to call a repository would be the service layer. If you adopt this layer, you might second-guess yourself when the service layer is a one-liner call to the repository because this is where it feels like an unneeded layer. The minute you have the service layer calling a repository, taking the results, and calling a behavior, it provides a more readable function because it is orchestrating the fetching of the data and the application of business logic.

Orchestrations

In a small application where there is a single entry point (e.g., a controller), the controller is often treated like an orchestrator. It is responsible for calling one service, taking the results of that, and potentially calling another service.

In the current application that is being built, orchestrations aren't required yet because the controllers are only calling the same single service. If this were to expand, introducing the orchestration layer would make a lot of sense.

The orchestration layer allows your controller to focus on its job, which is to convert data from the request and convert data for the response.

Unit of Work

With ORMs like Entity Framework, when you query data from the database, the ORM is tracking the data in its internal context. EF uses this to know whether the data has changed and what data it needs to update when the transaction is committed. Similarly, before you commit a transaction when you are adding a new record, it needs to be added to EF's context.

In the previous examples shown over the past few chapters, the `AuthorsController` marks the `Author` model as added, modified, or deleted. This is followed by a call to the `SaveChanges` function. No data is ever persisted to the database until this function is called.

Enter the Unit of Work pattern. By maintaining a single Unit of Work throughout the entire request, different services can insert or manipulate data. When the business transaction is done, the owner of the Unit of Work can commit the final transaction.

Picking the layer that owns the Unit of Work is based on complexity. You need to decide which layer knows when the final business transaction is completed. The layer that has this context is the layer that should own the Unit of Work.

For example, if you implement all of the layers, starting with a controller communicating with an orchestrator, an orchestrator communicating with one or more services, and then a service communicating with one or more repositories and one or more behaviors, the owner of the Unit of Work would then be the orchestrator. The service understands when it has finished its job, but it is unaware if there are other side effects that will be executed afterward.

In the next section, because this is a small application, I will demonstrate integrating the service and behavior layer only. In this scenario, I have deemed the service to be the owner of the Unit of Work because it knows when the business transaction is completed.

Figure 12-1 demonstrates how the Unit of Work encapsulates the entire business transaction that is owned by the orchestrator.

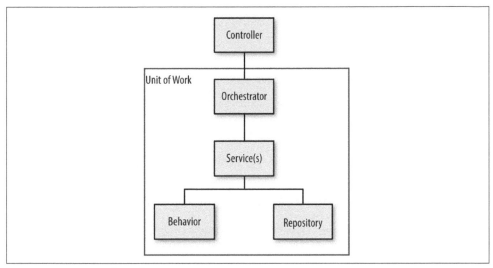

Figure 12-1. Unit of Work

Services and Behaviors

There has been a bit too much copying and pasting for me, and I'm starting to find the controllers to be disorganized. This section will refactor the two `AuthorsControl lers` and split the work into one service and one behavior. The `BookContext` will also be completely removed from the `AuthorsController` and now owned by the service.

The first piece of work that needs to be refactored is the duplicated logic to get a list of authors. Example 12-1 contains the code in question.

Example 12-1. Duplicated retrieval of authors

```
var start = (queryOptions.CurrentPage - 1) * queryOptions.PageSize;
var authors = db.Authors.
    OrderBy(queryOptions.Sort).
    Skip(start).
    Take(queryOptions.PageSize);

queryOptions.TotalPages =
    (int)Math.Ceiling((double)db.Authors.Count() / queryOptions.PageSize);
```

Let's start with the behavior. The block of code performs two different calculations. You can guarantee that if you were to build another controller that contained a list of objects, these calculations would need to be made again.

Example 12-2 creates a new class called `QueryOptionsCalculator`. For organization purposes, I have created a new folder called `Behaviors` and placed the class within it.

Example 12-2. QueryOptionsCalculator

```
using BootstrapIntroduction.ViewModels;
using System;

namespace BootstrapIntroduction.Behaviors
{
  public class QueryOptionsCalculator
  {
    public static int CalculateStart(QueryOptions queryOptions)
    {
      return (queryOptions.CurrentPage - 1) * queryOptions.PageSize;
    }

    public static int CaclulateTotalPages(int count, int pageSize)
    {
      return (int)Math.Ceiling((double)count / pageSize);
    }
  }
}
```

The class contains two functions, one for each calculation that was in Example 12-1.

Now it's time for the service. Example 12-3 creates a new AuthorService class. Once again for organization purposes, I have created a new *Services* folder and placed this class within it.

Example 12-3. AuthorService

```
using BootstrapIntroduction.Behaviors;
using BootstrapIntroduction.DAL;
using BootstrapIntroduction.Models;
using BootstrapIntroduction.ViewModels;
using System;
using System.Collections.Generic;
using System.Data.Entity;
using System.Linq;
using System.Linq.Dynamic;
using System.Net;
using System.Web;
using System.Web.Mvc;

namespace BootstrapIntroduction.Services
{
  public class AuthorService
  {
    private BookContext db = new BookContext();

    public List<Author> Get(QueryOptions queryOptions)
    {
      var start = QueryOptionsCalculator.CalculateStart(queryOptions);
```

```
        var authors = db.Authors.
          OrderBy(queryOptions.Sort).
          Skip(start).
          Take(queryOptions.PageSize);

        queryOptions.TotalPages = QueryOptionsCalculator.CaclulateTotalPages(
          db.Authors.Count(), queryOptions.PageSize);

        return authors.ToList();
      }
    }
}
```

The `AuthorService` contains a function called `Get` that accepts the `QueryOptions` class. The two calculations are replaced with calls to the new behavior created in Example 12-2. The same query that was previously in the controllers is now done in the `Get` function.

To complete the removal of the `BookContext` from the `AuthorsController`, the `AuthorService` must implement four other functions: `GetById`, `Insert`, `Update`, and `Delete`. Also, previously the `BookContext` was being disposed via the controller. The `AuthorService` will thus implement the `IDisposable` interface and properly dispose of the `BookContext`. The dispose function of `AuthorService` will then be called by the `AuthorsController`. Example 12-4 contains the complete `AuthorService`.

Example 12-4. Completed AuthorService

```
using BootstrapIntroduction.Behaviors;
using BootstrapIntroduction.DAL;
using BootstrapIntroduction.Models;
using BootstrapIntroduction.ViewModels;
using System;
using System.Collections.Generic;
using System.Data.Entity;
using System.Linq;
using System.Linq.Dynamic;
using System.Net;
using System.Web;
using System.Web.Mvc;

namespace BootstrapIntroduction.Services
{
  public class AuthorService : IDisposable
  {
    private BookContext db = new BookContext();

    public List<Author> Get(QueryOptions queryOptions)
    {
```

```
    var start = QueryOptionsCalculator.CalculateStart(queryOptions);

    var authors = db.Authors.
      OrderBy(queryOptions.Sort).
      Skip(start).
      Take(queryOptions.PageSize);

    queryOptions.TotalPages = QueryOptionsCalculator.CaclulateTotalPages(
      db.Authors.Count(), queryOptions.PageSize);

    return authors.ToList();
  }

  public Author GetById(long id)
  {
    Author author = db.Authors.Find(id);
    if (author == null)
    {
      throw new System.Data.Entity.Core.ObjectNotFoundException
        (string.Format("Unable to find author with id {0}", id));
    }

    return author;
  }

  public void Insert(Author author)
  {
    db.Authors.Add(author);

    db.SaveChanges();
  }

  public void Update(Author author)
  {
    db.Entry(author).State = EntityState.Modified;

    db.SaveChanges();
  }

  public void Delete(Author author)
  {
    db.Authors.Remove(author);

    db.SaveChanges();
  }

  public void Dispose() {
    db.Dispose();
  }
  }
}
```

With the `AuthorService` completed, the two `AuthorControllers` can be updated to remove the `BookContext` and replace it with the `AuthorService`. Example 12-5 contains the updated MVC `AuthorsController`.

Example 12-5. Updated MVC AuthorsController

```
using System;
using System.Collections.Generic;
using System.Net;
using System.Web;
using System.Web.ModelBinding;
using System.Web.Mvc;
using BootstrapIntroduction.Models;
using BootstrapIntroduction.ViewModels;
using BootstrapIntroduction.Filters;
using BootstrapIntroduction.Services;

namespace BootstrapIntroduction.Controllers
{
  public class AuthorsController : Controller
  {
    private AuthorService authorService;

    public AuthorsController()
    {
      authorService = new AuthorService();

      AutoMapper.Mapper.CreateMap<Author, AuthorViewModel>();
    }

    // GET: Authors
    [GenerateResultListFilterAttribute(typeof(Author), typeof(AuthorViewModel))]
    public ActionResult Index([Form] QueryOptions queryOptions)
    {
      var authors = authorService.Get(queryOptions);

      ViewData["QueryOptions"] = queryOptions;

      return View(authors);
    }

    // GET: Authors/Details/5
    public ActionResult Details(int? id)
    {
      if (id == null)
      {
        return new HttpStatusCodeResult(HttpStatusCode.BadRequest);
      }

      var author = authorService.GetById(id.Value);
```

```csharp
    return View(AutoMapper.Mapper.Map<Author, AuthorViewModel>(author));
}

// GET: Authors/Create
[BasicAuthorization]
public ActionResult Create()
{
  return View("Form", new AuthorViewModel());
}

// GET: Authors/Edit/5
[BasicAuthorization]
public ActionResult Edit(int? id)
{
  if (id == null)
  {
    return new HttpStatusCodeResult(HttpStatusCode.BadRequest);
  }

  var author = authorService.GetById(id.Value);

  return View("Form", AutoMapper.Mapper.Map<Author, AuthorViewModel>(author));
}

// GET: Authors/Delete/5
[BasicAuthorization]
public ActionResult Delete(int? id)
{
  if (id == null)
  {
    return new HttpStatusCodeResult(HttpStatusCode.BadRequest);
  }

  var author = authorService.GetById(id.Value);

  return View(AutoMapper.Mapper.Map<Author, AuthorViewModel>(author));
}

// POST: Authors/Delete/5
[HttpPost, ActionName("Delete")]
[ValidateAntiForgeryToken]
[BasicAuthorization]
public ActionResult DeleteConfirmed(int id)
{
  var author = authorService.GetById(id);

  authorService.Delete(author);

  return RedirectToAction("Index");
}

protected override void Dispose(bool disposing)
```

```
    {
      if (disposing)
      {
        authorService.Dispose();
      }
      base.Dispose(disposing);
    }
  }
}
```

Previously, the `AuthorsController` was calling `Dispose` on the `BookContext`. Like everything else in the controller that was referencing `BookContext`, it has been replaced with a call to dispose of the `AuthorService`.

Dispose

Disposing of the `BookContext` is important to ensure that any open database connections are properly closed at the end of each request. Leaving orphaned database connections can lead to eventual database connection problems because it is normal to allow only a limited number of concurrent connections.

There is one other small refactoring within the controllers—the automapping has been moved to the constructor instead of repeating this in each action. The fewer lines of code, the easier your application is to maintain.

Example 12-6 contains the final piece of implementing the fat model, which is to update the Web API `AuthorsController`.

Example 12-6. Web API AuthorsController

```
using System;
using System.Collections.Generic;
using System.Net;
using System.Net.Http;
using System.Web.Http;
using System.Web.Http.Description;
using BootstrapIntroduction.Models;
using BootstrapIntroduction.ViewModels;
using BootstrapIntroduction.Services;

namespace BootstrapIntroduction.Controllers.Api
{
  public class AuthorsController : ApiController
  {
    private AuthorService authorService;

    public AuthorsController()
    {
```

```csharp
  authorService = new AuthorService();

  AutoMapper.Mapper.CreateMap<Author, AuthorViewModel>();
  AutoMapper.Mapper.CreateMap<AuthorViewModel, Author>();
}

// GET: api/Authors
public ResultList<AuthorViewModel> Get([FromUri]QueryOptions queryOptions)
{
  var authors = authorService.Get(queryOptions);

  return new ResultList<AuthorViewModel>(
    AutoMapper.Mapper.Map<List<Author>, List<AuthorViewModel>>(authors)
      , queryOptions);
}

// GET: api/Authors/5
[ResponseType(typeof(AuthorViewModel))]
public IHttpActionResult Get(int id)
{
  var author = authorService.GetById(id);

  return Ok(AutoMapper.Mapper.Map<Author, AuthorViewModel>(author));
}

// PUT: api/Authors/5
[ResponseType(typeof(void))]
public IHttpActionResult Put(AuthorViewModel author)
{
  var model = AutoMapper.Mapper.Map<AuthorViewModel, Author>(author);

  authorService.Update(model);

  return StatusCode(HttpStatusCode.NoContent);
}

// POST: api/Authors
[ResponseType(typeof(AuthorViewModel))]
public IHttpActionResult Post(AuthorViewModel author)
{
  var model = AutoMapper.Mapper.Map<AuthorViewModel, Author>(author);

  authorService.Insert(model);

  return CreatedAtRoute("DefaultApi", new { id = author.Id }, author);
}

// DELETE: api/Authors/5
[ResponseType(typeof(Author))]
public IHttpActionResult DeleteAuthor(int id)
{
  var author = authorService.GetById(id);
```

```
      authorService.Delete(author);

      return Ok(author);
    }

    protected override void Dispose(bool disposing)
    {
      if (disposing)
      {
        authorService.Dispose();
      }
      base.Dispose(disposing);
    }
  }
}
```

Summary

I'm very happy with the resulting `AuthorsController`. Replacing the `BookContext` with the `AuthorService` has made both controllers extremely lean.

This chapter presented you with a possibility of implementing up to six layers of fat model and skinny controller. The examples implemented three of them (controller, service, and behavior). In a small project, all six layers would contain unnecessary class overhead; however, if you are working in a much larger project, you will find that you will need all six layers (and possibly more).

What I have found to be successful is to start with the minimum number of layers to separate your concerns properly. As your project evolves and grows, add the new layers as required. I've often added new layers only to new features and continually evolve the old code as changes are required. Quite often, you don't have time to globally implement a new layer, but there is no harm in continuing with a structure that is no longer working for you and slowly changing it over time.

PART IV

A Practical Example

CHAPTER 13

Building a Shopping Cart

This final section will bring together everything that has been previously demonstrated, as well as a variety of new things, into one large example. By the end of this section, we will have built a fully functional shopping cart.

Shopping Cart Requirements

Before building anything, I prefer to start with a definition of what I am going to build. The shopping cart that I will build will be targeted at buying books. I envision four different pages that a user can navigate:

Home page
> The home page (all pages actually) will contain a list of categories that will help filter the genre of books. This will be displayed on the left-hand side. The right-hand side will be used to display several featured books. Clicking a book will direct the user to the book details page.

Books by category
> If a user clicks a category on the left-hand side, a list of books in that category will be displayed (similar to how featured books are displayed). Clicking a book will direct the user to the book details page.

Book details
> The book details page is where users will go when they select a book. This page will display some basic information about the book and the all-important "Add to Cart" feature.

Cart details

> Once an item is added to the cart, the cart details page will display all items currently in the user's cart. This page will allow the user to edit the quantity or remove the item from the cart.

Using a shared layout, the category listing will be displayed on every page, allowing the user to find a different book quickly. A cart summary will be displayed in the top menu that will contain a visible indicator of how many items are currently in the user's cart. Clicking the icon will display a small summary of the items in the cart with a link to the cart details page.

Bootstrap will be used to create a nice user interface for the shopping cart. Knockout.js will be used to provide a slick user interface when adding/editing/deleting items from the cart. And, of course, MVC 5 will be used to enable the catalog of books to be stored/retrieved from a database.

The Shopping Cart Project

In the first three parts of this book, you have been extending a single project. For this final example, I have decided to make a new project; however, I will be leveraging many of the existing code created in the previous project.

With Visual Studio open, click File → New Project. Just like in Chapter 1, select the ASP.NET Web Application template. For the project name, I have chosen Shopping Cart. Select OK to continue. Once again, for the Web Templates, you will select the MVC template. This time, select the Web API checkbox as well, because Web API controllers will be leveraged in building the various AJAX endpoints. I have chosen No authentication because this example will be focusing on the CRUD of a shopping cart and not require authentication.

Once your new project is created, I would suggest that you immediately open the NuGet Package Manager and update all currently installed NuGet packages.

With the NuGet Package Manager still open, you need to install several new packages:

- Knockout.js
- Entity Framework
- Automapper

jQuery UI will also be used to perform some basic animations when items are added and removed from the user's shopping cart. Visit the jQuery UI website (*http://jquery.com*) to download the latest version. Once downloaded, I added it to the *Scripts* folder of my project.

JavaScript Bundling and Minification

Before we got started with creating the shopping cart, I want to touch upon JavaScript bundling. You may have noticed that in the original layout, jQuery was slightly different from Knockout and other JavaScript ViewModels that were created.

jQuery was included with a bundle that was generated by C# when the project was compiled, thus it was included like this: `@Scripts.Render("~/bundles/jquery")`. Other scripts were included like this: `@Scripts.Render("~/Scripts/knockout-3.2.0.js")`. The latter contains a relative path to the full JavaScript filename. The former contains the name of the bundle.

Bundles are defined in the *BundleConfig.cs* file inside the *App_Start* folder. Example 13-1 contains the default config file that is created with the project.

Example 13-1. Default BundleConfig

```
using System.Web;
using System.Web.Optimization;

namespace ShoppingCart
{
    public class BundleConfig
    {
        // For more information on bundling, visit http://go.microsoft.com/fwlink
        public static void RegisterBundles(BundleCollection bundles)
        {
            bundles.Add(new ScriptBundle("~/bundles/jquery").Include(
                "~/Scripts/jquery-{version}.js"));

            bundles.Add(new ScriptBundle("~/bundles/jqueryval").Include(
                "~/Scripts/jquery.validate*"));

            bundles.Add(new ScriptBundle("~/bundles/modernizr").Include(
                "~/Scripts/modernizr-*"));

            bundles.Add(new ScriptBundle("~/bundles/bootstrap").Include(
                "~/Scripts/bootstrap.js",
                "~/Scripts/respond.js"));

            bundles.Add(new StyleBundle("~/Content/css").Include(
                "~/Content/bootstrap.css",
                "~/Content/site.css"));

            // Set EnableOptimizations to false for debugging. For more information,
            // visit http://go.microsoft.com/fwlink/?LinkId=301862
            BundleTable.EnableOptimizations = true;
        }
    }
}
```

Creating a bundle requires adding a new ScriptBundle to the BundleCollection. The ScriptBundle requires two important things: a name and which files to include. The files to include can contain some logic to easily include more than one file. For example, the jqueryval bundle uses an asterisk (*) as a wildcard to include any file that contains the name *jquery.validate*.

My personal opinion is to create a single bundle with only the files required on most, if not all, pages. For this project, it will include jQuery, jQuery Validation, jQuery UI, Bootstrap, and Knockout. Example 13-2 contains an updated BundleConfig class that defines the single bundle to include in the shared layout view.

Example 13-2. Updated BundleConfig

```
using System.Web;
using System.Web.Optimization;

namespace ShoppingCart
{
  public class BundleConfig
  {
    // For more information on bundling, visit http://go.microsoft.com/fwlink
    public static void RegisterBundles(BundleCollection bundles)
    {
      bundles.Add(new ScriptBundle("~/bundles/shoppingCart").Include(
            "~/Scripts/jquery-{version}.js", "~/Scripts/jquery.validate*",
            "~/Scripts/jquery-ui.js", "~/Scripts/bootstrap.js",
            "~/Scripts/respond.js", "~/Scripts/knockout-{version}.js"));

      bundles.Add(new ScriptBundle("~/bundles/modernizr").Include(
            "~/Scripts/modernizr-*"));

      bundles.Add(new StyleBundle("~/Content/css").Include(
            "~/Content/bootstrap.css",
            "~/Content/site.css"));

      // Set EnableOptimizations to false for debugging. For more information,
      // visit http://go.microsoft.com/fwlink/?LinkId=301862
      BundleTable.EnableOptimizations = true;
    }
  }
}
```

The bundle was renamed to be shoppingCart, and I've comma-separated the six different JavaScript libraries that I want to be included on every page.

To complete the update, in *Views/Shared/_Layout.cshtml*, replace the previously added jQuery bundle with the new shoppingCart bundle using @Scripts.Ren der("~/bundles/shoppingCart").

Summary

The new `ShoppingCart` project is now created and updated with the necessary NuGet packages. Our requirements have been defined and will be implemented over the next several chapters.

CHAPTER 14

Building the Data Model

Once again, Entity Framework will be used as the ORM of choice for fetching and saving data for the shopping cart. This chapter will create the Code-First data models, instantiate some sample data, and create the necessary ViewModels that will be used by the MVC application.

Code-First Models

I am envisioning five models that will be required for the shopping cart:

Author model
> This model will contain information about the book's author.

Book model
> This model will contain information about the book being sold, including things like the price, an author foreign key, and a category foreign key.

Category model
> This model will contain an ID and name of the category. Each book will belong to one category (for simplicity).

Cart model
> This model will contain a unique identifier of the user who owns the shopping cart. Each visitor to the site will be associated to a Cart model.

CartItem model
> This model will contain which book and how many are being purchased. This object is a child to the Cart model.

The following examples contain these model definitions, as well as their inter-relationships with each other. Inside the *Models* folder, one file per model can be created. I've named each file the same as the class name.

Example 14-1 contains the `Author` model, which introduces a new feature of Entity Framework with the attribute `NotMapped`. I have created a `FullName` variable, which concantenates the first and last name into a single variable. By tagging the property with the attribute, EF knows that this property should not be persisted to the database. The `FullName` property will be used by the ViewModel that will be created in a later section.

Example 14-1. Author model

```
using System.Collections.Generic;
using System.ComponentModel.DataAnnotations.Schema;

namespace ShoppingCart.Models
{
  public class Author
  {
    public int Id { get; set; }
    public string FirstName { get; set; }
    public string LastName { get; set; }
    public string Biography { get; set; }

    [NotMapped]
    public string FullName
    {
      get
      {
        return FirstName + ' ' + LastName;
      }
    }

    public virtual ICollection<Book> Books { get; set; }
  }
}
```

Example 14-2 contains the `Book` model. This model has been expanded from the earlier version used to include pricing information, as well as a Boolean to indicate whether the book will be featured on the home page.

Example 14-2. Book model

```
namespace ShoppingCart.Models
{
  public class Book
  {
    public int Id { get; set; }
```

```
    public int AuthorId { get; set; }
    public int CategoryId { get; set; }
    public string Title { get; set; }
    public string Isbn { get; set; }
    public string Synopsis { get; set; }
    public string Description { get; set; }
    public string ImageUrl { get; set; }
    public decimal ListPrice { get; set; }
    public decimal SalePrice { get; set; }
    public bool Featured { get; set; }

    public virtual Author Author { get; set; }
    public virtual Category Category { get; set; }
  }
}
```

Example 14-3 contains the `Category` model, which contains an ID, name, and a collection of books that are associated with this category.

Example 14-3. Category model

```
using System.Collections.Generic;
namespace ShoppingCart.Models
{
  public class Category
  {
    public int Id { get; set; }
    public string Name { get; set; }

    public virtual ICollection<Book> Books { get; set; }
  }
}
```

The `Cart` model (shown in Example 14-4) is much like the `Category` model in that it contains only an `Id`, `SessionId`, and a collection of the associated cart items. The `Ses sionId` is the unique identifier that will be used to identify who owns the cart.

Example 14-4. Cart model

```
using System.Collections.Generic;
using System.ComponentModel.DataAnnotations;
using System.ComponentModel.DataAnnotations.Schema;

namespace ShoppingCart.Models
{
  public class Cart
  {
    public int Id { get; set; }

    [Index(IsUnique=true)]
```

```
    [StringLength(255)]
    public string SessionId { get; set; }

    public virtual ICollection<CartItem> CartItems { get; set; }
  }
}
```

The `SessionId` is also decorated with two EF attributes. The first attribute identifies that this property should be created as a unique index. Because this field will be searched on for each page load to find the user's cart, this is a good performance improvement. The second attribute defines a maximum string length. By default, if no string length is identified, EF will create string fields as `nvarchar(max)`, and an index is not compatible with this type of field.

And finally, Example 14-5 contains the `CartItem` model definition. Apart from tracking the quantity of books being purchased, this table contains nothing but relationships to the cart and the book being purchased.

Example 14-5. CartItem model

```
namespace ShoppingCart.Models
{
  public class CartItem
  {
    public int Id { get; set; }
    public int CartId { get; set; }
    public int BookId { get; set; }
    public int Quantity { get; set; }

    public virtual Cart Cart { get; set; }
    public virtual Book Book { get; set; }
  }
}
```

Defining the DbContext and Initializing Data

Before the data models will be used, several additional Entity Framework setup steps are required. Just like I did in Chapter 4, I have created a new *DAL* (Data Access Layer) folder and created my `ShoppingCartContext` file that defines my five datasets (as shown in Example 14-6).

Example 14-6. ShoppingCartContext

```
using ShoppingCart.Models;
using System.Data.Entity;
using System.Data.Entity.ModelConfiguration.Conventions;

namespace ShoppingCart.DAL
```

```
{
  public class ShoppingCartContext : DbContext
  {
    public DbSet<Category> Categories { get; set; }
    public DbSet<Book> Books { get; set; }
    public DbSet<Author> Authors { get; set; }
    public DbSet<Cart> Carts { get; set; }
    public DbSet<CartItem> CartItems { get; set; }

    protected override void OnModelCreating(DbModelBuilder modelBuilder)
    {
      modelBuilder.Conventions.Remove<PluralizingTableNameConvention>();

      base.OnModelCreating(modelBuilder);
    }
  }
}
```

To ensure that I have some data to test out my shopping cart with, I have a created a
`DataInitialization` class (also inside the *DAL* folder) that will create some books,
authors, and categories as shown in Example 14-7.

Example 14-7. DataInitialization

```
using ShoppingCart.Models;
using System.Collections.Generic;
using System.Data.Entity;

namespace ShoppingCart.DAL
{
  public class DataInitialization :
      DropCreateDatabaseIfModelChanges<ShoppingCartContext>
  {
    protected override void Seed(ShoppingCartContext context)
    {
      var categories = new List<Category>
      {
        new Category {
          Name = "Technology"
        },
        new Category {
          Name = "Science Fiction"
        },
        new Category {
          Name = "Non Fiction"
        },
        new Category {
          Name = "Graphic Novels"
        }
      };
```

```
categories.ForEach(c => context.Categories.Add(c));

var author = new Author
{
  Biography = "...",
  FirstName = "Jamie",
  LastName = "Munro"
};

var books = new List<Book>
{
  new Book {
    Author = author,
    Category = categories[0],
    Description = "...",
    Featured = true,
    ImageUrl =
        "http://ecx.images-amazon.com/images/I/51T%2BWt430bL._AA160_.jpg",
    Isbn = "1491914319",
    ListPrice = 19.99m,
    SalePrice = 17.99m,
    Synopsis = "...",
    Title = "Knockout.js: Building Dynamic Client-Side Web Applications"
  },
  new Book {
    Author = author,
    Category = categories[0],
    Description = "...",
    Featured = true,
    ImageUrl = "http://ecx.images-amazon.com/images/I/51AkFkNeUxL._AA160_.jpg",
    Isbn = "1449319548",
    ListPrice = 14.99m,
    SalePrice = 13.99m,
    Synopsis = "...",
    Title = "20 Recipes for Programming PhoneGap"
  },
  new Book {
    Author = author,
    Category = categories[0],
    Description = "...",
    Featured = false,
    ImageUrl = "http://ecx.images-amazon.com/images/I/51LpqnDq8-L._AA160_.jpg",
    Isbn = "1449309860",
    ListPrice = 19.99m,
    SalePrice = 16.99m,
    Synopsis = "...",
    Title = "20 Recipes for Programming MVC 3: Faster, Smarter Web Development"
  },
  new Book {
    Author = author,
    Category = categories[0],
    Description = "...",
```

```
            Featured = false,
            ImageUrl = "http://ecx.images-amazon.com/images/I/41JC54HEroL._AA160_.jpg",
            Isbn = "1460954394",
            ListPrice = 14.99m,
            SalePrice = 13.49m,
            Synopsis = "...",
            Title = "Rapid Application Development With CakePHP"
        }
    };

    books.ForEach(b => context.Books.Add(b));

    context.SaveChanges();
    }
  }
}
```

I've created four categories, one author, and four books. The four books are all related to the first category created, as well as the one author created. All of these objects are added to the corresponding EF dataset prior to calling SaveChanges to save the nine objects in the database.

To ensure that the database is initialized upon first start, the *Global.asax.cs* file inside the root of the project requires updating, as shown in Example 14-8, to initialize the database.

Example 14-8. Global.asax.cs

```
using ShoppingCart.DAL;
using System;
using System.Collections.Generic;
using System.Data.Entity;
using System.Linq;
using System.Web;
using System.Web.Http;
using System.Web.Mvc;
using System.Web.Optimization;
using System.Web.Routing;

namespace ShoppingCart
{
  public class MvcApplication : System.Web.HttpApplication
  {
    protected void Application_Start()
    {
      AreaRegistration.RegisterAllAreas();
      GlobalConfiguration.Configure(WebApiConfig.Register);
      FilterConfig.RegisterGlobalFilters(GlobalFilters.Filters);
      RouteConfig.RegisterRoutes(RouteTable.Routes);
      BundleConfig.RegisterBundles(BundleTable.Bundles);
```

```
        var dbContext = new ShoppingCartContext();
        Database.SetInitializer(new DataInitialization());
        dbContext.Database.Initialize(true);
    }

    protected void Session_Start(object sender, EventArgs e)
    {
        HttpContext.Current.Session.Add("__MyAppSession", string.Empty);
    }
  }
}
```

Example 14-8 also includes a new `Session_Start` function. Because the `SessionId` string in the Cart model will contain that user's HTTP Session ID, ASP.NET requires that the session be initialized with something. Typically, this would be accomplished if some user information were saved and retrieved on each request from the session; however, no data needs to be stored in the session, so instead, I just initialize with an empty string.

This appears to be a minor flaw in ASP.NET, because if this isn't done, the `SessionId` appears to be reset at random points.

The ViewModels

The ViewModels are almost identical to the models with a few minor adjustments to some of them. Just like the models, there are five ViewModels that serve much the same as their counterparts. The following examples contain the five different View-Models. I have created a new folder called *ViewModels* and have named the files the same as their class names. In each case, it is the name of the model postfixed by ViewModel. This helps separate them when the controller needs to work with both the data models and the ViewModels.

Example 14-9 contains the `AuthorViewModel`. You will notice that there are no fields for the first and last name, just the concantenated full name. This is a good example where the ViewModel only contains the full name because that is how it will always be used by the views created later.

Example 14-9. AuthorViewModel

```
using Newtonsoft.Json;
namespace ShoppingCart.ViewModels
{
  public class AuthorViewModel
  {
    [JsonProperty(PropertyName="id")]
    public int Id { get; set; }
```

```
    [JsonProperty(PropertyName = "fullName")]
    public string FullName { get; set; }

    [JsonProperty(PropertyName = "biography")]
    public string Biography { get; set; }
  }
}
```

The `BookViewModel` is shown in Example 14-10. For the most part, the fields match identically to the `Book` model with the exception of a calculated field called `SavePer centage`. This field performs a math calculation that will determine the difference (in percentage) between the sale and list price of the book. This will allow a view to list a savings percentage to the user.

Example 14-10. BookViewModel

```
using Newtonsoft.Json;
namespace ShoppingCart.ViewModels
{
  public class BookViewModel
  {
    [JsonProperty(PropertyName = "id")]
    public int Id { get; set; }

    [JsonProperty(PropertyName = "title")]
    public string Title { get; set; }

    [JsonProperty(PropertyName = "isbn")]
    public string Isbn { get; set; }

    [JsonProperty(PropertyName = "synopsis")]
    public string Synopsis { get; set; }

    [JsonProperty(PropertyName = "description")]
    public string Description { get; set; }

    [JsonProperty(PropertyName = "imageUrl")]
    public string ImageUrl { get; set; }

    [JsonProperty(PropertyName = "listPrice")]
    public decimal ListPrice { get; set; }

    [JsonProperty(PropertyName = "salePrice")]
    public decimal SalePrice { get; set; }

    [JsonProperty(PropertyName = "featured")]
    public bool Featured { get; set; }

    [JsonProperty(PropertyName = "savePercentage")]
    public int SavePercentage
```

```
    {
      get
      {
        return (int)(100 - (SalePrice / ListPrice * 100));
      }
    }

    [JsonProperty(PropertyName = "author")]
    public virtual AuthorViewModel Author { get; set; }

    [JsonProperty(PropertyName = "category")]
    public virtual CategoryViewModel Category { get; set; }
  }
}
```

Example 14-11 contains the `CategoryViewModel` that has been stripped down from its `Category` model to not include the list of books because the view that uses this ViewModel does not need to display the books.

Example 14-11. CategoryViewModel

```
using Newtonsoft.Json;

namespace ShoppingCart.ViewModels
{
  public class CategoryViewModel
  {
    [JsonProperty(PropertyName = "id")]
    public int Id { get; set; }

    [JsonProperty(PropertyName = "name")]
    public string Name { get; set; }
  }
}
```

The `CartViewModel` (shown in Example 14-12) does not include the `SessionId` because this is the server's unique identifier that does not need to be exposed publicly.

Example 14-12. CartViewModel

```
using Newtonsoft.Json;
using System.Collections.Generic;

namespace ShoppingCart.ViewModels
{
  public class CartViewModel
  {
    [JsonProperty(PropertyName = "id")]
    public int Id { get; set; }
```

```
    [JsonProperty(PropertyName = "cartItems")]
    public virtual ICollection<CartItemViewModel> CartItems { get; set; }
  }
}
```

And finally, Example 14-13 contains the `CartItemViewModel`, which is almost identical to its data model with the exception that data validation has been added to the `Quantity` property. The `Range` attribute forces the property to be within a min and max value. I have specified 1 for the minimum and the max value for an `Int32`. I've also specified a custom error message that will be displayed to the users if they do not enter a valid quantity range.

Example 14-13. CartItemViewModel

```
using Newtonsoft.Json;
using System;
using System.ComponentModel.DataAnnotations;

namespace ShoppingCart.ViewModels
{
  public class CartItemViewModel
  {
    [JsonProperty(PropertyName = "id")]
    public int Id { get; set; }

    [JsonProperty(PropertyName = "cartId")]
    public int CartId { get; set; }

    [JsonProperty(PropertyName = "bookId")]
    public int BookId { get; set; }

    [JsonProperty(PropertyName = "quantity")]
    [Range(1, Int32.MaxValue, ErrorMessage="Quantity must be greater than 0")]
    public int Quantity { get; set; }

    [JsonProperty(PropertyName = "book")]
    public BookViewModel Book { get; set; }
  }
}
```

Summary

The shopping cart project is starting to come together nicely. The database has been fully designed, created, and populated with some initial seed data. The next chapter will begin to create the layout for the shopping cart, including several items that will appear on every page of the site.

CHAPTER 15

Implementing the Layout

The shopping cart project is now fully prepared and ready to be implemented. This chapter will implement the two common elements that will be on each page of the site. The first is the menu of book categories, and the second is the cart summary that will allow the users to see a snapshot of what is in their cart.

The Shared Layout

When the shopping cart project was created by Visual Studio, it also created a Home Controller (along with the accompanying views) and a shared layout view. Example 15-1 contains an updated *Views/Shared/_Layout.cs* file that includes the two common elements.

Example 15-1. Shared layout

```
<!DOCTYPE html>
<html>
<head>
  <meta charset="utf-8" />
  <meta name="viewport" content="width=device-width, initial-scale=1.0">
  <title>@ViewBag.Title - My ASP.NET Application</title>
  @Styles.Render("~/Content/css")
  @Scripts.Render("~/bundles/modernizr")
</head>
<body>
  <div class="navbar">
    <div class="container">
      <div class="navbar-header">
        <button type="button" class="navbar-toggle"
                       data-toggle="collapse" data-target=".navbar-collapse">
          <span class="icon-bar"></span>
          <span class="icon-bar"></span>
```

```
          <span class="icon-bar"></span>
        </button>
        @Html.ActionLink("Jamie's Shopping Cart", "Index", "Home",
                    new { area = "" }, new { @class = "navbar-brand" })
      </div>
      <div class="navbar-collapse collapse">
        <ul class="nav navbar-nav">
          <li>@Html.ActionLink("Home", "Index", "Home")</li>
          <li>@Html.ActionLink("About", "About", "Home")</li>
          <li>@Html.ActionLink("Contact", "Contact", "Home")</li>
        </ul>
        <div class="navbar-right" id="cart-details">
          @Html.Action("Summary", "Carts")
        </div>
      </div>
    </div>
  </div>
  <div class="container body-content">
    <div class="well well-lg col-lg-3">
      @Html.Action("Menu", "Categories",
    new { selectedCategoryId = ViewBag.SelectedCategoryId != null ?
        ViewBag.SelectedCategoryId : 0 })
    </div>
    <div class="col-lg-9">
      @RenderBody()
    </div>
    <hr />
    <footer>
      <p>&copy; @DateTime.Now.Year - My ASP.NET Application</p>
    </footer>
  </div>

  @Scripts.Render("~/bundles/shoppingCart")
  @RenderSection("scripts", required: false)
</body>
</html>
```

The cart summary has been added to the top menu. After the three scaffolded links
for Home, About, and Contact, the cart summary is aligned on the far right. It is
implemented by using the HtmlHelper and calling the Action method. The input to
this function is the action and controller name that should be called by the MVC
framework. The resulting view will be rendered inside the containing div. This is a
good method to separate code properly. As you can see, the controller that will be
executed is the CartsController (this will be created shortly) and the action of
Summary.

Similar to the cart summary, the menu of categories is included the same way, this
time calling the CategoriesController and the Menu action. This time, additional
data is passed into the Action function. A new dynamic object is created with a property called selectedCategoryId. This property is set by checking if there is a ViewBag

variable named `SelectedCategoryId`. The `CategoriesController` will use this variable to be able to highlight the category the user has selected.

The category menu is placed inside the main container, which has been split into two columns. The first column will use up 3/12ths of the screen to display the categories. The second column will use the remaining 9/12ths to display the body of the page being rendered.

The Cart Summary

Several different pieces need to be created and put together to make the fully functional interactive cart summary. Example 15-2 is the `CartsController`, which is a new controller that should be added to the *Controllers* folder.

Example 15-2. CartsController

```
using ShoppingCart.Models;
using ShoppingCart.Services;
using ShoppingCart.ViewModels;
using System;
using System.Collections.Generic;
using System.Linq;
using System.Web;
using System.Web.Mvc;

namespace ShoppingCart.Controllers
{
  public class CartsController : Controller
  {
    private readonly CartService _cartService = new CartService();

    public CartsController()
    {
      AutoMapper.Mapper.CreateMap<Cart, CartViewModel>();
      AutoMapper.Mapper.CreateMap<CartItem, CartItemViewModel>();
      AutoMapper.Mapper.CreateMap<Book, BookViewModel>();
      AutoMapper.Mapper.CreateMap<Author, AuthorViewModel>();
      AutoMapper.Mapper.CreateMap<Category, CategoryViewModel>();
    }

    [ChildActionOnly]
    public PartialViewResult Summary()
    {
      var cart = _cartService.GetBySessionId(HttpContext.Session.SessionID);

      return PartialView(
        AutoMapper.Mapper.Map<Cart, CartViewModel>(cart)
      );
    }
```

```
      protected override void Dispose(bool disposing)
      {
        if (disposing)
        {
          _cartService.Dispose();
        }
        base.Dispose(disposing);
      }
    }
  }
```

The `CartsController` defines one public action called `Summary`, which is tagged with the attribute `ChildActionOnly`. This attribute, in combination with the layout loading this method via the `HtmlHelper` and the `Action` method, lets me use the MVC framework without the overhead of a full request.

The `CartsController` also instantiates a private variable to the `CartService` (shown in Example 15-3). This variable is then disposed of at the end of the request life cycle. The `Summary` method uses the `CartService` to get the cart by the user's `SessionID`, which is stored in the `HttpContext`.

Inside a new folder called *Services*, add the `CartService` class shown in Example 15-3

Example 15-3. CartService

```
using ShoppingCart.DAL;
using ShoppingCart.Models;
using System;
using System.Collections.Generic;
using System.Data.Entity;
using System.Linq;

namespace ShoppingCart.Services
{
  public class CartService : IDisposable
  {
    private ShoppingCartContext _db = new ShoppingCartContext();

    public Cart GetBySessionId(string sessionId)
    {
      var cart = _db.Carts.
        Include("CartItems").
        Where(c => c.SessionId == sessionId).
        SingleOrDefault();

      cart = CreateCartIfItDoesntExist(sessionId, cart);

      return cart;
    }
```

```
    private Cart CreateCartIfItDoesntExist(string sessionId, Cart cart)
    {
      if (null == cart)
      {
        cart = new Cart
        {
          SessionId = sessionId,
          CartItems = new List<CartItem>()
        };
        _db.Carts.Add(cart);
        _db.SaveChanges();
      }

      return cart;
    }

    public void Dispose()
    {
      _db.Dispose();
    }
  }
}
```

Just like I did with the previous service I created, a private variable is instantiated to the EF `DbContext`. This service implements the `IDisposable` interface, which will then dispose of the `ShoppingCartContext` when the controller's `Dispose` function is called to dispose of the `CartService`.

The `GetBySessionId` function searches the Carts `DbSet` for a cart with a matching `sessionId`. The `CartItems` collection is also included because this will be used by the view to show all of the items. Inside the `GetBySessionId` function is a private function named `CreateCartIfItDoesntExist`, which will create a new cart with the `sessionId` when there is not an existing cart.

Next up is the view. If a *Carts* folder was not created automatically under the *Views* folder, you should create it now. Once created, add a new view called `Summary`. Be sure to check that this is a partial view. Example 15-4 contains the finished `Summary` view.

Example 15-4. Carts/Summary.cshtml

```
@model ShoppingCart.ViewModels.CartViewModel
<a id="cart" href="@Url.Action("Index", "Carts")" data-bind="click: showCart">
  <span class="glyphicon glyphicon-shopping-cart"></span>
  <span class="badge" data-bind="text: cart.cartItems().length">
      @Model.CartItems.Count</span>
</a>
```

```
<div id="cart-summary" style="display: none">
  <span data-bind="visible: cart.cartItems().length == 0">
    You currently have no items in your cart.
  </span>
  <div data-bind="visible: cart.cartItems().length > 0">
    <ul>
      <!-- ko foreach: { data: cart.cartItems, afterAdd: fadeIn } -->
      <li data-bind="text: book.title"></li>
      <!-- /ko -->
    </ul>
    <p><strong>Total:</strong> $<span data-bind="text: cart.total"></span></p>
    <br /><a href="@Url.Action("Index", "Carts")" class="btn btn-primary">
        View cart details</a>
  </div>
</div>

<script>
  var cartSummaryData = @Html.HtmlConvertToJson(Model);
</script>
```

The `Summary` view is bound to the `CartViewModel` that was created in Chapter 14.
Remember that this view is included in the shared layout inside a class that aligns to
the far right. So this view defines an HTML link with an `id` of `cart` and a Knockout
data binding for the click event to the function `showCart`. Inside this link are two
`span` tags. The first one displays a shopping cart glyphicon. The second defines a
badge that is data bound via the `text` binding to the `cart.cartItems` array.

Beneath the link is a `div` with the `id` of `cart-summary`. It is hidden by default. When
the user clicks the shopping cart icon, this `div` will be displayed inside a popover.
Inside the `div`, a `span` tag is created and is data bound to the `visible` binding to show
when there are no items in the cart. Beneath this `span` tag is a `div` that is data bound
to the `visible` binding to only show when there are items in the cart. An unordered
list (`ul`) contains a `foreach` data binding, which creates a list item (`li`) with the title
of the book that is in the cart.

You might have noticed that the `foreach` binding looks different than some of the
previous bindings. I've indicated that after an item is added to the `cartItems` array,
an event will be triggered by Knockout and call the `fadeIn` function that will be
defined in the Knockout ViewModel. This will provide the ability to perform a little
animation when items are added to the cart.

Beneath the list of items in the cart is the cart's total and a link to view the full cart
details.

A global JavaScript variable is defined at the bottom of this view that serializes the
`CartViewModel`. Normally, the ViewModel would be instantiated here as well; however, here is a minor downside to using a partial view. Partial views don't support

sections, so I'm unable to define the scripts section that would be rendered at the bottom of the shared layout. Instead, when the CartSummaryViewModel is defined (as shown in Example 15-5), it will use this global variable that I've defined in this view.

I personally am not the biggest fan of using global JavaScript variables; however, in this scenario I think the pros of separating my code with a partial view and controller outweigh having to use a global JavaScript variable.

The Summary view is leveraging the HtmlHelperExtension that was created in Example 5-4. In the root of the project, create the *Extensions* folder and copy the previously created HtmlHelperExtension to this folder.

The cart summary is starting to come together, and now it's time to create the Knockout ViewModel. Inside the *Scripts* folder, create a new folder called *ViewModels*. Then create a new *CartSummaryViewModel.js* file as shown in Example 15-5.

Example 15-5. CartSummaryViewModel

```
function CartSummaryViewModel(model) {
  var self = this;

  self.cart = model;

  for (var i = 0; i < self.cart.cartItems.length; i++) {
    var cartItem = self.cart.cartItems[i];
    cartItem.quantity = ko.observable(cartItem.quantity)
                          .extend({ subTotal: cartItem.book.salePrice });
  }

  self.cart.cartItems = ko.observableArray(self.cart.cartItems);

  self.cart.total = self.cart.cartItems.total();

  self.showCart = function () {
    $('#cart').popover('toggle');
  };

  self.fadeIn = function (element) {
    setTimeout(function () {
      $('#cart').popover('show');

      $(element).slideDown(function () {
        setTimeout(function () {
          $('#cart').popover('hide');
        }, 2000);
      });
    }, 100);
  };

  $('#cart').popover({
```

```
    html: true,
    content: function () {
      return $('#cart-summary').html();
    },
    title: 'Cart Details',
    placement: 'bottom',
    animation: true,
    trigger: 'manual'
  });
};

if (cartSummaryData !== undefined) {
  var cartSummaryViewModel = new CartSummaryViewModel(cartSummaryData);
  ko.applyBindings(cartSummaryViewModel, document.getElementById("cart-details"));
} else {
  $('.body-content').prepend('<div class="alert alert-danger">
                <strong>Error!</strong> Could not find cart summary.</div>');
}
```

The `CartSummaryViewModel` is defined as a function that accepts the `CartViewModel` that was serialized in the view. This is assigned to a local `cart` variable. After this, the `cartItems` array is looped through, and the `quantity` property of the `CartItemView Model` is converted to an observable variable. This is required because if the same item is added multiple times, the quantity will be updated, and this will allow the cart total to be recalculated. The `cartItems` array is also converted to an `observableAr ray` because items will be added and removed from this array.

When the quantity is defined as an observable, it is extended with a `subTotal` property that passes in the book's `salePrice`. The `subTotal` is a custom Knockout extension that I created (shown in Example 15-6) that can be used to extend any observable property that will take the variable passed in and multiply it by the property that is being extended.

The `total` property on the cart variable is defined as a custom function on the `observableArray cartItems`. The `total` extension function is also shown in Example 15-6 below.

After the observables are created, the `showCart` function is defined. This function is bound to the click event for the cart icon and will toggle the display of the cart summary popover (i.e., if it is hidden, it will be shown, and when it is clicked again, it will be closed).

The next function is the `fadeIn` function. It accepts an `element` parameter that is passed by Knockout when the new item is added to the `cartItems` array. A `setTime out` is defined that will be executed 100 milliseconds after the function is called. This is done to ensure that the new element has been added to the list by Knockout. Once the 100 milliseconds have passed, the popover is shown (if it is not already being shown), and the jQuery UI `slideDown` effect will show the new item. After 2,000 milliseconds, the popover is then hidden. This provides a nice effect that shows the cart summary for roughly two seconds, and then disappears providing visual feedback to the user that the new item was added to the cart.

The final thing the `CartSummaryViewModel` function does is instantiate the link with the `id` of `cart` to be a popover. The popover is created with the title `Cart Details`, and the content is loaded from the `div` with the `id` of `cart-summary`.

Outside of the `CartSummaryViewModel` function, there is an `if` statement that ensures that the global JavaScript variable that was defined in the view exists. If it does exist, it creates the view model and applies the Knockout bindings limited to the element with the `id` of `cart-details`. The `cart-details` ID was added in the shared layout to the element that wraps the `Html.Action` method call. Limiting the Knockout bindings to only the content within the `cart-details` `div` allows you to add multiple Knockout bindings on the same page.

If the global variable doesn't exist, an error alert is written on-screen. This will help any future developer if this variable is not defined.

The next thing that needs to be created is the custom `subTotal` Knockout extension and `total` custom function. I've placed these in a file called *knockout.custom.js* inside the *Scripts* folder. Example 15-6 defines these functions.

Example 15-6. knockout.custom.js

```
ko.extenders.subTotal = function (target, multiplier) {
  target.subTotal = ko.observable();

  function calculateTotal(newValue) {
    target.subTotal((newValue * multiplier).toFixed(2));
  };

  calculateTotal(target());

  target.subscribe(calculateTotal);

  return target;
};

ko.observableArray.fn.total = function () {
  return ko.pureComputed(function () {
    var runningTotal = 0;

    for (var i = 0; i < this().length; i++) {
      runningTotal += parseFloat(this()[i].quantity.subTotal());
    }
```

```
        return runningTotal.toFixed(2);
    }, this);
};
```

The `subTotal` is defined as function under the `ko.extenders`. By default, the function will have one parameter, the target observable. This extender also includes a second property of `multiplier`. The function adds a new observable property called `subTotal` to the target observable. Then a function is defined called `calculateTotal`. This will be called each time the target observable's value changes. The `calculateTotal` function is called on first load and will be called automatically each time the value changes.

The `total` function is defined slightly differently. It is defined as a function on the `ko.observableArray`. By adding it here, it will be available to any `observableArray`. If it were added to the `ko.observable`, the function would be available to both `observable` and `observableArray` variables.

A `pureComputed` function is defined inside the function definition. This function loops through the `observableArray` and adds the results of the previously defined `subTotal` function to the `runningTotal` variable. At the end of this function, the `runningTotal` is returned fixed to two decimal places.

This `pureComputed` function will be recalculated when either the `cartItems` array changes or when the quantity within the `cartItem` changes.

Why Custom Functions?

Instead of creating an extension, the `subTotal` and `total` could be calculated with a `computedObservable`. I've gone with the extension approach because when I create the cart details page, it also needs to calculate the same `subTotal` and `total` for each cart item. This is a great way to avoid duplicating the calculation across multiple ViewModels.

The final thing that needs to be done is to include the new JavaScript files that have been created. This can be accomplished one of two ways. The first would be to include the scripts in the layout after the bundle created in Chapter 13 is added. The second way would be to update the previously created bundle to include these new files. Because these files are required on every page, I think it makes more sense to update the bundle with them. Example 15-7 contains an updated `BundleConfig` with the two additional files.

Example 15-7. Updated BundleConfig

```
using System.Web;
using System.Web.Optimization;

namespace ShoppingCart
{
  public class BundleConfig
  {
    // For more information on bundling, visit http://go.microsoft.com/fwlink
    public static void RegisterBundles(BundleCollection bundles)
    {
      bundles.Add(new ScriptBundle("~/bundles/shoppingCart").Include(
            "~/Scripts/jquery-{version}.js", "~/Scripts/jquery.validate*",
            "~/Scripts/jquery-ui.js", "~/Scripts/bootstrap.js",
            "~/Scripts/respond.js", "~/Scripts/knockout-{version}.js",
            "~/Scripts/knockout.custom.js",
            "~/Scripts/ViewModels/CartSummaryViewModel.js"));

      bundles.Add(new StyleBundle("~/Content/css").Include(
            "~/Content/bootstrap.css",
            "~/Content/site.css"));

      // Set EnableOptimizations to false for debugging. For more information,
      // visit http://go.microsoft.com/fwlink/?LinkId=301862
      BundleTable.EnableOptimizations = true;
    }
  }
}
```

At this point, the application can be run. Clicking the cart icon will display the popover with the message, "You currently have no items in your cart" (as shown in Figure 15-1).

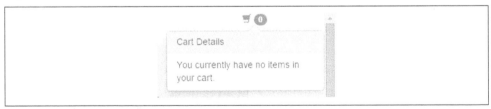

Figure 15-1. The cart summary

The Categories Menu

The list of categories is implemented in a similar fashion to the cart summary with far fewer pieces to put together. To begin, create a new CategoriesController in the *Controllers* folder. Example 15-8 contains its definition.

Example 15-8. CategoriesController

```
using ShoppingCart.Models;
using ShoppingCart.Services;
using ShoppingCart.ViewModels;
using System.Collections.Generic;
using System.Web;
using System.Web.Mvc;

namespace ShoppingCart.Controllers
{
  public class CategoriesController : Controller
  {
    private readonly CategoryService _categoryService = new CategoryService();

    [ChildActionOnly]
    public PartialViewResult Menu(int selectedCategoryId)
    {
      var categories = _categoryService.Get();

      AutoMapper.Mapper.CreateMap<Category, CategoryViewModel>();

      ViewBag.SelectedCategoryId = selectedCategoryId;

      return PartialView(
        AutoMapper.Mapper.Map<List<Category>, List<CategoryViewModel>>(categories)
      );
    }

    protected override void Dispose(bool disposing)
    {
      if (disposing)
      {
        _categoryService.Dispose();
      }
      base.Dispose(disposing);
    }
  }
}
```

The CategoriesController is following the same methodology of creating a service and ensuring that it is disposed of when the request is finished. The Menu action is also tagged as a ChildActionOnly like the Summary action in the CartsController.

Using the CategoryService (shown in Example 15-9), all categories are retrieved. These are then automapped and passed to the partial view (shown in Example 15-10). If you recall in the shared layout, when the Html.Action method was called, a new dynamic object was created to pass in the selectedCategoryId property. This value is set in the ViewBag to be used by the view to identify the selected category (if one is selected).

Example 15-9 contains the `CategoryService`. This file should be created in the *Services* folder.

Example 15-9. CategoryService

```
using ShoppingCart.DAL;
using ShoppingCart.Models;
using System;
using System.Collections.Generic;
using System.Linq;

namespace ShoppingCart.Services
{
  public class CategoryService : IDisposable
  {
    private ShoppingCartContext _db = new ShoppingCartContext();

    public List<Category> Get()
    {
      return _db.Categories.OrderBy(c => c.Name).ToList();
    }

    public void Dispose()
    {
      _db.Dispose();
    }
  }
}
```

The `CategoryService` follows the same paradigm as other services where it creates a new `ShoppingCartContext`, implements the `IDisposable` interface, and disposes of the `DbContext` when the class is disposed of from the controller.

The `Get` function simply returns the `DbSet` of `Categories` ordered alphabetically by their name.

The final piece to the category menu is the view. Inside the *Views* folder, if a *Categories* folder was not automatically created with the controller, add it now. Inside of this folder create a new view called `Menu`. Once again, ensure that the partial view is checked. Example 15-10 contains the view.

Example 15-10. Categories/Menu

```
@model List<ShoppingCart.ViewModels.CategoryViewModel>
@{
  var selectedCategoryId = ViewBag.SelectedCategoryId;
}

<div class="list-group">
```

```
    <h4 class="list-group-item-heading">Categories</h4>
@foreach (var category in Model)
{
  <a href="@Url.Action("Index", "Books", new { categoryId = category.Id })"
     class="list-group-item @if (selectedCategoryId == category.Id) {
         @Html.Raw("active") }">@category.Name</a>
}
</div>
```

The view is data bound to a list of `CategoryViewModels` and the `ViewBag.SelectedCa tegoryId` is stored in a local variable. A Razor `foreach` statement is placed within a `div` with the class of `list-group`. A new HTML link is created for each category. The link is assigned the class `list-group-item`, and if the ID of the category matches the `selectedCategoryId`, a secondary class of `active` is added. This class will highlight the selected menu. This is shown in Figure 15-2.

Figure 15-2. The categories

Where's the Knockout?

It's a good question. I have chosen Knockout to perform my client-side data binding; however, because I know the categories will not change when a user interacts with them, there is no need to add the additional override of Knockout bindings.

You will notice throughout the remainder of these examples that Knockout is only used when dynamic user interaction is required; otherwise, a standard MVC view with Razor will do the trick just fine.

Summary

The shopping cart layout is now complete. The list of book categories will be displayed on the left, and the cart summary will be displayed in the upper-right corner. These items will appear on every page. The cart summary contains a nice mix of MVC, Bootstrap, and Knockout to style it as a popover and include some simple animations when new items are added to the cart. The next chapter will build the home page to include a list of featured books.

CHAPTER 16

Lists of Books

This chapter will update the home page to display a list of featured books. Because the Book model contained both a list price and sale price, a savings label will be added to attract the user into buying the book! Another list of books needs to be displayed filtered to the category selected from the left-hand menu created in Chapter 15. Both the featured books and the filtered-by-category books will leverage a shared view as shown later in this chapter.

The Home Page

Before the books are displayed, I've made some minor changes to the home page that was previously scaffolded by Visual Studio. Example 16-1 contains the updated *Views/Home/Index.cshtml* view with the tweaks.

Example 16-1. Views/Home/Index.cshtml

```
@{
    ViewBag.Title = "Home Page";
}

<div class="jumbotron">
    <h1>Jamie's Shopping Cart</h1>
    <p class="lead">Shop for your favorite books, we've got the best prices.</p>
    <p><a href="@Url.Action("About")" class="btn btn-primary btn-lg">
        Learn more &raquo;</a></p>
</div>

@Html.Action("Featured", "Books")
```

The view leverages the stylish jumbotron feature of Bootstrap. This is a great way to create a noticable call-to-action that users cannot miss. My jumbotron is quite simple in that it tells the users I have the best prices, and they can click a link to learn more.

After the jumbotron, the featured books are included via the `Html.Action` method, just like the cart summary and categories were included in the shared layout. This was done to leverage both a `HomeController` and a `BooksController` and keep each related to their respective objects. The next section will implement the featured books.

No changes are required to the `HomeController` because it does not contain any logic. It simply loads the view.

The Featured Books

To create the featured books, create a `BooksController` inside the *Controllers* folder. Example 16-2 contains the `Featured` action of the `BooksController`.

Example 16-2. BooksController

```
using ShoppingCart.Models;
using ShoppingCart.Services;
using ShoppingCart.ViewModels;
using System;
using System.Collections.Generic;
using System.Web;
using System.Web.Mvc;

namespace ShoppingCart.Controllers
{
  public class BooksController : Controller
  {
    private readonly BookService _bookService = new BookService();

    public BooksController()
    {
      AutoMapper.Mapper.CreateMap<Book, BookViewModel>();
      AutoMapper.Mapper.CreateMap<Author, AuthorViewModel>();
      AutoMapper.Mapper.CreateMap<Category, CategoryViewModel>();
    }

    [ChildActionOnly]
    public PartialViewResult Featured()
    {
      var books = _bookService.GetFeatured();

      return PartialView(
        AutoMapper.Mapper.Map<List<Book>, List<BookViewModel>>(books)
      );
```

```
    }

    protected override void Dispose(bool disposing)
    {
      if (disposing)
      {
        _bookService.Dispose();
      }
      base.Dispose(disposing);
    }
  }
}
```

Hopefully, the BooksController is looking quite familiar. I have once again followed the previously defined pattern. A BookService is instantiated (shown in Example 16-3) and is disposed of at the end of the request.

Next is the Featured action. Just like the cart summary and categories menu, this action is attributed with ChildActionOnly. The Featured action uses the BookService to retrieve the list of featured books. These books are then automapped to the BookViewModel and passed through to the view (shown in Example 16-4).

The BookService class can now be created inside the existing Services folder. Example 16-3 contains the BookService with the GetFeatured method.

Example 16-3. BookService

```
using ShoppingCart.DAL;
using ShoppingCart.Models;
using System;
using System.Collections.Generic;
using System.Linq;
using System.Web;

namespace ShoppingCart.Services
{
  public class BookService : IDisposable
  {
    private ShoppingCartContext _db = new ShoppingCartContext();

    public List<Book> GetFeatured()
    {
      return _db.Books.
        Include("Author").
        Where(b => b.Featured).
        ToList();
    }

    public void Dispose()
    {
```

```
      _db.Dispose();
    }
  }
}
```

Like the previous services, the `BookService` implements the `IDisposable` interface and creates a `ShoppingCartContext` that is disposed of when the request is finished.

The `GetFeatured` method returns a list of books with the `Featured` Boolean set to true. The related `Author` object is also included so that it can be rendered along with the book.

It's now time to create the view. If a `Books` folder was not created in the *Views* folder, create it now. Inside this folder create a new *Featured* view. Be sure to check the partial view because this is a Child Action Only view. Example 16-4 contains the nearly empty view (because the logic is contained within another shared view that is shown in Example 16-5).

Example 16-4. Views/Books/Featured.cshtml

```
@model List<ShoppingCart.ViewModels.BookViewModel>
@Html.Partial("_List", Model)
```

This view defines the model binding a list of `BookViewModels`. After this, another `HtmlHelper` method is used—`Partial`—that defines the name of the partial view to load. The second parameter is the optional data that the partial view can be data bound to.

The final piece of the featured books is the HTML code to list the books. In the *Views/Books* folder, create another partial view named *_List*. The underscore in the name is a common convention to help identify partial views not associated directly with a controller action. Example 16-5 shows the *_List.cshtml* view.

Example 16-5. Views/Books/_List.cshtml

```
@model List<ShoppingCart.ViewModels.BookViewModel>
@{
  const int maxPerRow = 3;
  int counter = 0;
}

<div class="row">
  @foreach (var book in Model)
  {
    counter++;
    if (counter > maxPerRow)
    {
      counter = 0;
```

```
@Html.Raw("</div>")
@Html.Raw("<div class=\"row\">")
    }
    <div class="col-md-4">
      <a href="@Url.Action("Details", "Books", new { book.Id })" class="thumbnail">
        <img src="@book.ImageUrl" alt="@book.Title" title="@book.Title" />
        <span class="label label-success">Save @book.SavePercentage %</span>
      </a>
      <h4><a href="@Url.Action("Details", "Books", new { book.Id })">
          @book.Title</a></h4>
      <p>@book.Author.FullName</p>
      <p>Your Price: $@book.SalePrice</p>
      <p>List Price: <span style="text-decoration: line-through">
          $@book.ListPrice</span></p>
    </div>
  }
</div>
```

Like the Featured view, this view is also data bound to a list of BookViewModels. After this, a couple of variables are defined that will help split the books into rows of three. Before looping through the list of books, a div with the class of row is defined. This div is closed after the end of the loop. During the loop of books, the counter is incremented. When the counter surpasses the maxPerRow, the div with the class of row is closed, and the new div is created.

Next up is creating the column with the book information. Another div is created with the class of col-md-4. This will make each book use up to one-third of the screen width. The book's thumbnail is added inside an HTML link. The image inside of the link is specially stylized because of the thumbnail class on the link. Under the image, a span tag is defined with the label and label-success classes that contain the book's savings percentage.

And finally, the book's title, author, and the prices are displayed with a strikethrough on the list price as shown in Figure 16-1.

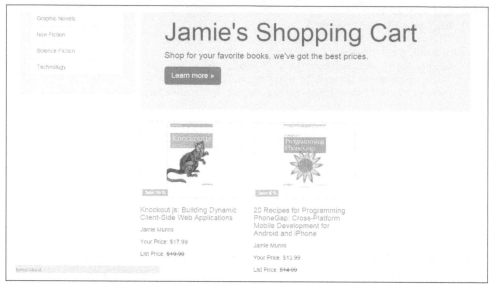

Figure 16-1. Featured books

Filtered Books by Category

In the last chapter when the category menu was created, each category was linked to the `Index` action on the `BooksController`. The link also provided the `categoryId`. Example 16-6 contains an updated `BooksController` with the new `Index` action.

Example 16-6. Updated BooksController

```
using ShoppingCart.Models;
using ShoppingCart.Services;
using ShoppingCart.ViewModels;
using System;
using System.Collections.Generic;
using System.Web;
using System.Web.Mvc;

namespace ShoppingCart.Controllers
{
  public class BooksController : Controller
  {
    private readonly BookService _bookService = new BookService();

    public BooksController()
    {
      AutoMapper.Mapper.CreateMap<Book, BookViewModel>();
      AutoMapper.Mapper.CreateMap<Author, AuthorViewModel>();
      AutoMapper.Mapper.CreateMap<Category, CategoryViewModel>();
    }
```

```
// GET: Books
public ActionResult Index(int categoryId)
{
  var books = _bookService.GetByCategoryId(categoryId);

  ViewBag.SelectedCategoryId = categoryId;

  return View(
    AutoMapper.Mapper.Map<List<Book>, List<BookViewModel>>(books)
  );
}

[ChildActionOnly]
public PartialViewResult Featured()
{
  var books = _bookService.GetFeatured();

  return PartialView(
    AutoMapper.Mapper.Map<List<Book>, List<BookViewModel>>(books)
  );
}

protected override void Dispose(bool disposing)
{
  if (disposing)
  {
    _bookService.Dispose();
  }
  base.Dispose(disposing);
}
  }
}
```

The Index method leverages the BookService to fetch the list of books by the cate
goryId parameter. This list is then automapped and passed through to the view.

Recall that in the shared layout, when the Html.Action to include the category menu
was called, the selectedCategoryId was populated with a ViewBag variable if it existed. This is the controller that sets the variable so that the selected category will be
highlighted when the view is rendered.

The BookService requires updating to include the new GetByCategoryId function.
This is shown in Example 16-7.

Example 16-7. Updated BookService

```
using ShoppingCart.DAL;
using ShoppingCart.Models;
using System;
```

```
using System.Collections.Generic;
using System.Linq;
using System.Web;

namespace ShoppingCart.Services
{
  public class BookService : IDisposable
  {
    private ShoppingCartContext _db = new ShoppingCartContext();

    public List<Book> GetByCategoryId(int categoryId)
    {
      return _db.Books.
        Include("Author").
        Where(b => b.CategoryId == categoryId).
        OrderByDescending(b => b.Featured).
        ToList();
    }

    public List<Book> GetFeatured()
    {
      return _db.Books.
        Include("Author").
        Where(b => b.Featured).
        ToList();
    }

    public void Dispose()
    {
      _db.Dispose();
    }
  }
}
```

The `GetByCategoryId` function is quite similar to the `GetFeatured` function; however, this time the books are filtered where their `CategoryId` is equal to the `categor yId` parameter. The `Author` object is also included, and to provide more upsell, the books with the `Featured` flag set to true are displayed first.

To finish displaying the books, an *Index* view needs to be created in the *Views/Books* folder. This time ensure that the partial view is not checked! The completed view is displayed in Example 16-8.

Example 16-8. Views/Books/Index.cshtml

```
@model List<ShoppingCart.ViewModels.BookViewModel>
@{
  ViewBag.Title = "Books";
}
```

```
<h2>Books</h2>

@if (Model.Count > 0) {
  @Html.Partial("_List", Model)
} else {
<div class="alert alert-info">
  There are currently no books to display.
</div>
}
```

Like the previously created book views, the `Index` view is also data bound to a list of `BookViewModels`. A Razor `if` statement is then used to show the partial `_List` view (shown in Example 16-5) to show the books. If there are no books, an alert is displayed letting the user know there are no books in this category.

When you run the completed example, you will see the category highlighted on the left, letting you easily know which category you are currently browsing.

Summary

Like the category menu, this entire chapter did not require any dynamic user interaction, so Knockout was not used. Bootstrap was leveraged throughout in an attempt to make the books visually appealing to the user with minimal effort.

Get ready for the next chapter. More Knockout will be required to add the ability to add a book to your shopping cart!

CHAPTER 17

Adding Items to the Cart

As my product owner at work likes to say, this is the chapter where "the rubber meets the road." The previous chapters have been providing the necessary setup before building the "why," and when it comes to shopping carts, the "why" is adding the item to the cart.

The Book Details

Before a book can be added to the cart, the book details page needs to be created. In the last chapter when the book listings were created, the link to the book sent the user to Books/Details/id. To start, the BooksController needs to be updated to add this new action. Example 17-1 contains an updated BooksController.

Example 17-1. Updated BooksController

```
using ShoppingCart.Models;
using ShoppingCart.Services;
using ShoppingCart.ViewModels;
using System;
using System.Collections.Generic;
using System.Web;
using System.Web.Mvc;

namespace ShoppingCart.Controllers
{
  public class BooksController : Controller
  {
    private readonly BookService _bookService = new BookService();

    public BooksController()
    {
      AutoMapper.Mapper.CreateMap<Book, BookViewModel>();
```

```
    AutoMapper.Mapper.CreateMap<Author, AuthorViewModel>();
    AutoMapper.Mapper.CreateMap<Category, CategoryViewModel>();
  }

  // GET: Books
  public ActionResult Index(int categoryId)
  {
    var books = _bookService.GetByCategoryId(categoryId);

    ViewBag.SelectedCategoryId = categoryId;

    return View(
      AutoMapper.Mapper.Map<List<Book>, List<BookViewModel>>(books)
    );
  }

  public ActionResult Details(int id)
  {
    var book = _bookService.GetById(id);

    return View(
      AutoMapper.Mapper.Map<Book, BookViewModel>(book)
    );
  }

  [ChildActionOnly]
  public PartialViewResult Featured()
  {
    var books = _bookService.GetFeatured();

    return PartialView(
      AutoMapper.Mapper.Map<List<Book>, List<BookViewModel>>(books)
    );
  }

  protected override void Dispose(bool disposing)
  {
    if (disposing)
    {
      _bookService.Dispose();
    }
    base.Dispose(disposing);
  }
}
}
```

The Details action is quite similar to the other actions in the BooksController. It uses the BookService to fetch an individual book by its ID. This book is then automapped to the view.

The BookService needs to be updated to include the new GetById function as shown in Example 17-2.

Example 17-2. Updated BookService

```
using ShoppingCart.DAL;
using ShoppingCart.Models;
using System;
using System.Collections.Generic;
using System.Linq;
using System.Web;

namespace ShoppingCart.Services
{
  public class BookService : IDisposable
  {
    private ShoppingCartContext _db = new ShoppingCartContext();

    public List<Book> GetByCategoryId(int categoryId)
    {
      return _db.Books.
        Include("Author").
        Where(b => b.CategoryId == categoryId).
        OrderByDescending(b => b.Featured).
        ToList();
    }

    public List<Book> GetFeatured()
    {
      return _db.Books.
        Include("Author").
        Where(b => b.Featured).
        ToList();
    }

    public Book GetById(int id)
    {
      var book = _db.Books.
        Include("Author").
        Where(b => b.Id == id).
        SingleOrDefault();

      if (null == book)
        throw new System.Data.Entity.Core.ObjectNotFoundException
          (string.Format("Unable to find book with id {0}", id));

      return book;
    }

    public void Dispose()
    {
```

```
        _db.Dispose();
    }
  }
}
```

Once again, the `BookService` updates are almost identical. This time instead of returning a list, it returns only a single book. There is an additional check to see if the book exists. If it does not, an exception is thrown.

To complete the display of the book, a *Details* view is required. Inside the *Views/Books* folder, create a new view called *Details*. Like the *Index* view, this should not be a partial view. Example 17-3 contains the finished view.

Example 17-3. Views/Books/Details.cshtml

```
@model ShoppingCart.ViewModels.BookViewModel
@{
  ViewBag.Title = Model.Title;
}

<h1>@Model.Title</h1>

<div id="bookDetails" class="row">
  <div class="col-md-2">
    <img src="@Model.ImageUrl" alt="@Model.Title" title="@Model.Title"
        class="img-rounded" />
  </div>
  <div class="col-md-5 col-md-offset-1">
    <h3>@Model.Author.FullName</h3>
    <p>Your Price: $@Model.SalePrice</p>
    <p>List Price: <span style="text-decoration: line-through">
        $@Model.ListPrice</span></p>
    <p class="label label-success">Save @Model.SavePercentage %</p>
    <p>@Model.Description</p>
  </div>
  <div class="col-md-2 col-md-offset-2 bg-info">
    <upsert-cart-item params="cartItem: cartItem, showButton: true">
        </upsert-cart-item>
  </div>
</div>

@Html.Partial("_CartItemForm")

@section Scripts {
  @Scripts.Render("~/Scripts/ViewModels/BookDetailViewModel.js",
    "~/Scripts/ViewModels/CartItemViewModel.js")

  <script>
    var model = @Html.HtmlConvertToJson(Model);

    var bookDetailViewModel = new BookDetailViewModel(model);
```

```
      ko.applyBindings(bookDetailViewModel, document.getElementById("bookDetails"));
   </script>
}
```

There is quite a bit going on inside this view. First, the view is data bound to a single BookViewModel. After this, the page title is set to the name of the book, and this is also displayed inside a header (h1).

After this, the main book details are displayed inside a div attributed with the id of bookDetails. At the end of the view, the Knockout BookDetailViewModel is data bound to this div. The Knockout ViewModel will be described in the next section.

Inside this div, the book thumbnail, author, description, and pricing information are displayed. The book details are split into three columns. The first and second contain the preceding information. The last column contains the form to add the book to the cart. This is accomplished by using a custom Knockout component. I've named the component upsert-cart-item because it is also used on the cart details page that will be implemented in the next chapter.

The upsert-cart-item component accepts two parameters: the first is the item being added or edited (hence the term *upsert*), and the second parameter is a Boolean variable that indicates whether or not the form's button should always be displayed. When the cart details page is implemented, the button will only be shown when the book's quantity changes.

The final part of the *Details* view is to include the partial view that will be used by the Knockout component, load the necessary JavaScript files, and create an instance of the ViewModel with the BookViewModel.

Inside the *Scripts/ViewModels* folder, create a new *BookDetailViewModel.js* JavaScript file as shown in Example 17-4.

Example 17-4. BookDetailViewModel

```
function BookDetailViewModel(model) {
  var self = this;

  self.cartItem = {
    cartId: cartSummaryViewModel.cart.id,
    quantity: ko.observable(1),
    book: model
  };
};
```

This ViewModel accepts the BookViewModel, which is bound to a book property inside the cartItem variable. This ViewModel also leverages the global cartSummary ViewModel to set the cartId for the cartItem. The quantity property is made observable to allow the user to change this value to order more copies. The `cartItem` variable is the object that is data bound to the Knockout custom component that will be reviewed in the next section. Figure 17-1 is an example of a fully functional book details page.

Figure 17-1. Book details

Custom Components and Custom Bindings

The previous section set everything in place to show the book details and the add-to-cart form. The add-to-cart was accomplished using a custom Knockout component. Inside the component, a custom Knockout binding is also used to show or hide the Submit button. This is a nice effect when the cart details page is implemented because the Update button will only show when the quantity has been changed.

Knockout custom components are quite powerful. They let you encapsulate both HTML and a Knockout ViewModel together in a standalone and reusable component. To create a component, you need three things:

A unique name
    The custom component I created is called `upsert-cart-item`.

A ViewModel
    The ViewModel can be inline or an existing ViewModel. I've chosen the latter for better organization.

A template
    The template can be inline, or it can reference a template by ID. I've chosen the latter once again for better organization.

To start, the component needs to be registered with Knockout. Example 17-5 contains the code required to register my component.

Example 17-5. Component registration

```
ko.components.register('upsert-cart-item', {
  viewModel: CartItemViewModel,
  template: { element: 'cart-item-form' }
});
```

The ViewModel that the component uses is called `CartItemViewModel` (shown in Example 17-6), and the template parameter identifies that Knockout should use the element with the `id` of `cart-item-form`. This will be shown in Example 17-7.

Inside the *Scripts/ViewModels* folder, create a new JavaScript file called `CartItemView Model`. The class is shown in Example 17-6. Notice at the bottom of this file is where I placed the component registration from Example 17-5.

Example 17-6. CartItemViewModel

```
function CartItemViewModel(params) {
  var self = this;

  self.sending = ko.observable(false);

  self.cartItem = params.cartItem;
  self.showButton = params.showButton;

  self.upsertCartItem = function (form) {
    if (!$(form).valid())
      return false;

    self.sending(true);

    var data = {
      id: self.cartItem.id,
      cartId: self.cartItem.cartId,
      bookId: self.cartItem.book.id,
      quantity: self.cartItem.quantity()
    };

    $.ajax({
      url: '/api/cartitems',
      type: self.cartItem.id === undefined ? 'post' : 'put',
      contentType: 'application/json',
      data: ko.toJSON(data)
    })
    .success(self.successfulSave)
    .error(self.errorSave)
    .complete(function () { self.sending(false) });
  };

  self.successfulSave = function (data) {
    var msg = '<div class="alert alert-success"><strong>Success!</strong>
```

```
      The item has been ';
    if (self.cartItem.id === undefined)
      msg += 'added to';
    else
      msg += 'updated in';

    $('.body-content').prepend(msg + ' your cart.</div>');

    self.cartItem.id = data.id;

    cartSummaryViewModel.updateCartItem(ko.toJS(self.cartItem));
  };

  self.errorSave = function () {
    var msg = '<div class="alert alert-danger"><strong>Error!</strong>
        There was an error ';
    if (self.cartItem.id === undefined)
      msg += 'adding';
    else
      msg += 'updating';

    $('.body-content').prepend(msg + ' the item to your cart.</div>');
  };
};

ko.components.register('upsert-cart-item', {
  viewModel: CartItemViewModel,
  template: { element: 'cart-item-form' }
});
```

The ViewModel accepts a params parameter. This contains the objects passed into the component as they were named when the component was added. These are then stored into local copies—one for the cartItem being added or edited, and the other for whether or not the button should always show.

The upsertCartItem function is defined next. This is called when the form is submitted. It first checks that the form is valid, and then the sending observable is set to true; this will make the progress bar show. After this, a new variable named data is defined. This builds the object that will be sent to the server with only the information that is required by the server. This is not mandatory, but is a good thing to do because if you recall, the cartItem object contains the full book object, and there is no need to send this information to the server.

This function finishes by performing the AJAX request. The endpoint it calls is api/cartItems (this controller will be created shortly). Depending on whether the cartItem is being added or edited, it will either perform a POST or PUT request, respectively. The data is then serialized to JSON, and finally, the success and error functions are set for when the request finishes. At the completion of the AJAX request (regardless of success or fail), the `sending` observable is set back to false to hide the progress bar.

The `successfulSave` function is called when the cart item is successfully saved. This function builds a message to identify whether the item was added or updated in the cart. This message is then displayed in a success alert near the top of the screen. The final thing this function does is call a new function in the global `cartSummaryViewMo del`. The function accepts the `cartItem` that was just added or edited.

The final function in this class is the `errorSave` function. This function builds and displays an error alert if the save is not successful.

That completes the component's ViewModel. It's now time to create the template. I've placed the template in a partial view called _CartItemForm_ (shown in Example 17-7). Because this will be used by both a view in the *Books* folder and the future *CartItems* folder, I created the _CartItemForm_ in the *Shared* folder under *Views*.

Example 17-7. Views/Shared/_CartItemForm.cshtml

```
@{
  var cartItem = new ShoppingCart.ViewModels.CartItemViewModel();
}

<template id="cart-item-form">
  <form class="center-block" data-bind="submit: upsertCartItem">
    <div class="form-group">
      <!-- ko if: cartItem.id === undefined -->
      @Html.LabelFor(m => cartItem.Quantity)
      <!-- /ko -->
      <div class="input-group form-group-sm">
        <div class="col-sm-8">
          @Html.TextBoxFor(m => cartItem.Quantity,
                new { data_bind = "textInput: cartItem.quantity",
                  @class = "form-control" })
          @Html.ValidationMessageFor(m => cartItem.Quantity, "",
                new { @class = "text-danger" })
        </div>
      </div>
    </div>
    <div class="form-group" data-bind="isDirty: cartItem.quantity">
      <button type="submit" class="btn btn-primary" data-bind="visible: !sending(),
            text: cartItem.id === undefined ? 'Add To Cart' : 'Update'"></button>
    </div>
  </form>

  <div class="progress" data-bind="visible: sending">
    <div class="progress-bar progress-bar-info progress-bar-striped active"
        role="progressbar" aria-valuenow="100"
        aria-valuemin="0" aria-valuemax="100"
        style="width: 100%">
```

```
      <span class="sr-only"></span>
    </div>
  </div>
</template>
```

The view begins by instantiating the `CartItemViewModel` class. This will be used to strongly bind the form to it when using the `HtmlHelper`.

The HTML begins by defining the `template` tag with the ID that matches the component registration, `cart-item-form`. Inside the template is the HTML to build the form. The form is data bound on the submit event to the `upsertCartItem` function defined in the ViewModel. Next, if this is being used to add an item to the cart, a quantity label is created. When this is used on the cart details page, it will be in a table with a header identifying that the form is for the quantity. Then the textbox is created. It is data bound to the `cartItem` quantity property. Instead of using the `value` data binding, it is using the `textInput` data binding. This acts quite similarly to the other binding, with the exception that Knockout tracks every character change and not just when the textbox loses focus. This helps provide instant feedback to the `isDirty` data binding that will be discussed next.

To complete the form, the submit button is added. It contains a conditional attribute to display the text "Add to Cart" or "Update" depending on whether the item is being added or updated. The button is contained within a `div` that has a custom Knockout binding called `isDirty` on it. The `isDirty` binding extends the `visible` binding to hide the button when editing until the quantity has changed.

The view is completed with a progress bar that is displayed when the `sending` observable is set to true.

Example 17-8 contains the custom `isDirty` binding. I've placed this in the existing *knockout.custom.js file.*

Example 17-8. Updated knockout.custom.js

```
ko.bindingHandlers.isDirty = {
  init: function (element, valueAccessor, allBindings, viewModel, bindingContext) {
    var originalValue = ko.unwrap(valueAccessor());

    var interceptor = ko.pureComputed(function () {
      return (bindingContext.$data.showButton !== undefined &&
          bindingContext.$data.showButton)
          || originalValue != valueAccessor()();
    });

    ko.applyBindingsToNode(element, {
      visible: interceptor
    });
  }
```

```
};

ko.extenders.subTotal = function (target, multiplier) {
  target.subTotal = ko.observable();

  function calculateTotal(newValue) {
    target.subTotal((newValue * multiplier).toFixed(2));
  };

  calculateTotal(target());

  target.subscribe(calculateTotal);

  return target;
};

ko.observableArray.fn.total = function () {
  return ko.pureComputed(function () {
    var runningTotal = 0;

    for (var i = 0; i < this().length; i++) {
      runningTotal += parseFloat(this()[i].quantity.subTotal());
    }

    return runningTotal.toFixed(2);
  }, this);
};
```

The isDirty binding is added to the ko.bindingHandlers. It contains an init property that is defined as a function. This function accepts five parameters: the element that is being data bound, the property the binding is attached to, all other bindings on this element, the ViewModel (this is being deprecated), and the binding context. This is the new way to access the ViewModel.

Inside the init function, the starting quantity value is stored to a variable. After this, a pureComputed observable is defined that returns true or false, depending on whether the button should be shown or hidden. It will return true when the showBut ton variable is set to true or when the originalValue does not equal the current value. This observable is then used to tell Knockout that this binding extends the visible binding.

This same logic could be applied to the visible binding directly; however, creating the custom binding is much cleaner and reusable.

The CartItemViewModel called a function in the global CartSummaryViewModel. Example 17-9 contains an updated CartSummaryViewModel with the updateCartItem function.

Example 17-9. Updated CartSummaryViewModel

```javascript
function CartSummaryViewModel(model) {
  var self = this;

  self.cart = model;

  for (var i = 0; i < self.cart.cartItems.length; i++) {
    var cartItem = self.cart.cartItems[i];
    cartItem.quantity = ko.observable(cartItem.quantity)
                    .extend({ subTotal: cartItem.book.salePrice });
  }

  self.cart.cartItems = ko.observableArray(self.cart.cartItems);

  self.cart.total = self.cart.cartItems.total();

  self.updateCartItem = function (cartItem) {
    var isNewItem = true;

    for (var i = 0; i < self.cart.cartItems().length; i++) {
      if (self.cart.cartItems()[i].id == cartItem.id) {
        self.cart.cartItems()[i].quantity(cartItem.quantity);
        isNewItem = false;
        break;
      }
    }

    if (isNewItem) {
      cartItem.quantity = ko.observable(cartItem.quantity)
                    .extend({ subTotal: cartItem.book.salePrice });
      self.cart.cartItems.push(cartItem);
    }
  };

  self.showCart = function () {
    $('#cart').popover('toggle');
  };

  self.fadeIn = function (element) {
    setTimeout(function () {
      $('#cart').popover('show');

      $(element).slideDown(function () {
        setTimeout(function () {
          $('#cart').popover('hide');
        }, 2000);
      });
    }, 100);
  };

  $('#cart').popover({
```

```
    html: true,
    content: function () {
      return $('#cart-summary').html();
    },
    title: 'Cart Details',
    placement: 'bottom',
    animation: true,
    trigger: 'manual'
  });
};

if (cartSummaryData !== undefined) {
  var cartSummaryViewModel = new CartSummaryViewModel(cartSummaryData);
  ko.applyBindings(cartSummaryViewModel, document.getElementById("cart-details"));
} else {
  $('.body-content').prepend('<div class="alert alert-danger">
              <strong>Error!</strong> Could not find cart summary.</div>');
}
```

This function accepts the newly added or edited `cartItem` as input. The existing `cartItems` array is looped through to see if the same item was added again. If it was, `quantity` is updated to the quantity in the updated `cartItem`. If it doesn't already exist, the item is added to the end of the `cartItems` array. This will trigger the previously defined `fadeIn` function.

This completes the custom Knockout component and data binding. The next section will finish the add-to-cart process by defining the `CartItemsController`.

Saving the Cart Item

Because the add-to-cart is accomplished via AJAX, the saving will leverage a WebAPI controller to accept and return JSON data instead of full HTML forms and views. To begin, create an *Api* folder inside the *Controllers* folder and add a new WebAPI controller called `CartItemsController` to it (as shown in Example 17-10).

Example 17-10. CartItemsController

```
using ShoppingCart.Models;
using ShoppingCart.Services;
using ShoppingCart.ViewModels;
using System;
using System.Collections.Generic;
using System.Linq;
using System.Net;
using System.Net.Http;
using System.Web.Http;

namespace ShoppingCart.Controllers.Api
{
```

```
public class CartItemsController : ApiController
{
  private readonly CartItemService _cartItemService = new CartItemService();

  public CartItemsController()
  {
    AutoMapper.Mapper.CreateMap<Cart, CartViewModel>();
    AutoMapper.Mapper.CreateMap<CartItem, CartItemViewModel>();
    AutoMapper.Mapper.CreateMap<Book, BookViewModel>();

    AutoMapper.Mapper.CreateMap<CartItemViewModel, CartItem>();
    AutoMapper.Mapper.CreateMap<BookViewModel, Book>();
    AutoMapper.Mapper.CreateMap<AuthorViewModel, Author>();
    AutoMapper.Mapper.CreateMap<CategoryViewModel, Category>();
  }

  public CartItemViewModel Post(CartItemViewModel cartItem)
  {
    var newCartItem = _cartItemService.AddToCart(
                AutoMapper.Mapper.Map<CartItemViewModel, CartItem>(cartItem));

    return AutoMapper.Mapper.Map<CartItem, CartItemViewModel>(newCartItem);
  }

  protected override void Dispose(bool disposing)
  {
    if (disposing)
    {
      _cartItemService.Dispose();
    }
    base.Dispose(disposing);
  }
}
}
```

Unlike the previous controllers, because this is a WebAPI controller, it extends the
ApiController instead of the Controller. Otherwise, this controller follows the
same pattern. It creates a CartItemService and disposes of it when the request is finished.

Previously, the other controllers have contained Automapper definitions from the
Model to the ViewModel. This controller also contains definitions from the ViewModel to the Model because it does two-way mapping: once on the input and again on
the output.

The Post method calls the AddToCart function in the CartService and then returns
the newCartItem (after it is mapped from a Model to a ViewModel). The Put and
Delete methods will be created in the next chapter when the cart details can be
edited.

The CartItemService should be added as a class to the *Services* folder. It is defined in Example 17-11.

Example 17-11. CartItemService

```
using ShoppingCart.DAL;
using ShoppingCart.Models;
using System;
using System.Collections.Generic;
using System.Data.Entity;
using System.Linq;

namespace ShoppingCart.Services
{
  public class CartItemService : IDisposable
  {
    private ShoppingCartContext _db = new ShoppingCartContext();

    public CartItem GetByCartIdAndBookId(int cartId, int bookId)
    {
      return _db.CartItems.SingleOrDefault(ci => ci.CartId == cartId &&
          ci.BookId == bookId);
    }

    public CartItem AddToCart(CartItem cartItem)
    {
      var existingCartItem = GetByCartIdAndBookId(cartItem.CartId, cartItem.BookId);

      if (null == existingCartItem)
      {
        _db.Entry(cartItem).State = EntityState.Added;
        existingCartItem = cartItem;
      }
      else
      {
        existingCartItem.Quantity += cartItem.Quantity;
      }

      _db.SaveChanges();

      return existingCartItem;
    }

    public void Dispose()
    {
      _db.Dispose();
    }
  }
}
```

Like all other services, the `CartItemService` implements the `IDisposable` interface to properly dispose of the `ShoppingCartContext` that is created as a private variable.

The `GetByCartIdAndBookId` function accepts the `cartId` and `bookId` as parameters. The `CartItems DbSet` is then searched for a matching `CartItem`. This function is used by the `AddToCart` function to determine if the book being added already exists in the user's cart.

The `AddToCart` function calls `GetByCartIdAndBookId`. If there is no existing cart item, it is added to the `CartItems DbSet`, and the previously unset `existingCartItem` variable is set to the `cartItem` parameter because it will be used as the return value of the function. When there is an existing cart item, the quantity of that object is increased with the new quantity specified. After this, the changes are persisted to the database, and the `existingCartItem` is returned.

A book can now be successfully added to a user's shopping cart. The next chapter will both leverage and extend upon this code to allow users to edit or delete items in their cart.

Summary

The shopping cart is really taking shape now. This chapter extended Knockout with custom components and data bindings to create reusable functionality that will be leveraged in the next chapter to complete the shopping cart.

CHAPTER 18

Updating and Deleting Cart Items

To complete a usable shopping cart experience, this chapter will extend upon the previous examples to add functionality that will allow the user to increase the quantity of an item purchased or to remove the item completely.

The Cart Details

When the cart summary was created, a link was added to view the full details. That link defined the action as the `Index` of the `CartsController`. Example 18-1 updates the `CartsController` to add the new `Index` method.

Example 18-1. Updated CartsController

```
using ShoppingCart.Models;
using ShoppingCart.Services;
using ShoppingCart.ViewModels;
using System;
using System.Collections.Generic;
using System.Linq;
using System.Web;
using System.Web.Mvc;

namespace ShoppingCart.Controllers
{
  public class CartsController : Controller
  {
    private readonly CartService _cartService = new CartService();

    public CartsController()
    {
      AutoMapper.Mapper.CreateMap<Cart, CartViewModel>();
      AutoMapper.Mapper.CreateMap<CartItem, CartItemViewModel>();
```

```
    AutoMapper.Mapper.CreateMap<Book, BookViewModel>();
    AutoMapper.Mapper.CreateMap<Author, AuthorViewModel>();
    AutoMapper.Mapper.CreateMap<Category, CategoryViewModel>();
  }

  // GET: Carts
  public ActionResult Index()
  {
    var cart = _cartService.GetBySessionId(HttpContext.Session.SessionID);

    return View(
      AutoMapper.Mapper.Map<Cart, CartViewModel>(cart)
    );
  }

  [ChildActionOnly]
  public PartialViewResult Summary()
  {
    var cart = _cartService.GetBySessionId(HttpContext.Session.SessionID);

    return PartialView(
      AutoMapper.Mapper.Map<Cart, CartViewModel>(cart)
    );
  }

  protected override void Dispose(bool disposing)
  {
    if (disposing)
    {
      _cartService.Dispose();
    }
    base.Dispose(disposing);
  }
  }
}
```

The Index function is nearly identical to the previously created Summary with two key differences. First, it's not attributed with ChildActionOnly, and second, it returns a regular view and not a partial one. Otherwise, they use the same CartService function and automap to the same CartViewModel.

Unlike previous controller updates, no service updates are required because it is using an existing function. The *Index* view can now be created inside the *Views/Carts* folder. It should not be a partial view. Example 18-2 contains the new view.

Example 18-2. Views/Carts/Index.cshtml

```
@model ShoppingCart.ViewModels.CartViewModel
@{
  ViewBag.Title = "Cart Details";
```

```
}

<h2>Cart Details</h2>

<div id="cartDetails">
  <table class="table table-bordered table-hover table-striped"
    style="display:none" data-bind="visible:cart.cartItems().length > 0">
    <tr>
      <th>Book</th>
      <th>Unit Price</th>
      <th>Quantity</th>
      <th>Price</th>
      <th> </th>
    </tr>
    <!-- ko foreach: { data: cart.cartItems, beforeRemove: fadeOut } -->
    <tr>
      <td>
        <a href="@Url.Action("Details", "Books")"
                    data-bind="appendToHref: book.id, text: book.title"></a>
      </td>
      <td data-bind="text: '$' + book.salePrice"></td>
      <td>
        <upsert-cart-item params="cartItem: $data, showButton: false">
            </upsert-cart-item>
      </td>
      <td data-bind="text: '$' + quantity.subTotal()"></td>
      <td>
        <button type="button" class="btn btn-danger"
                data-bind="click: $parent.deleteCartItem, visible:
                    !$parent.sending()">
                <span class="glyphicon glyphicon-trash"></span></button>
      </td>
    </tr>
    <!-- /ko -->
  </table>

  <div class="progress" data-bind="visible: sending">
    <div class="progress-bar progress-bar-info progress-bar-striped active"
        role="progressbar" aria-valuenow="100"
        aria-valuemin="0" aria-valuemax="100"
        style="width: 100%">
      <span class="sr-only"></span>
    </div>
  </div>

  <div class="alert alert-warning" style="display: none"
            data-bind="visible: cart.cartItems().length == 0">
    Your cart is currently empty.
<a href="@Url.Action("Index", "Home")">Continue shopping</a>.
  </div>

  <h3>Total: $<span data-bind="text: cart.total"></span></h3>
```

```
</div>

@Html.Partial("_CartItemForm")

@section Scripts {
  @Scripts.Render("~/Scripts/ViewModels/CartDetailViewModel.js",
    "~/Scripts/ViewModels/CartItemViewModel.js")

  <script>
    var model = @Html.HtmlConvertToJson(Model);

    var cartDetailViewModel = new CartDetailViewModel(model);
    ko.applyBindings(cartDetailViewModel, document.getElementById("cartDetails"));
  </script>
}
```

Like the cart summary view, this view is also data bound to the `CartViewModel`. The HTML begins by defining a `div` tag with the `id` of `cartDetails`. The Knockout bindings will be applied to this `div`. Inside this `div`, a table is defined that will show each cart item. The table contains a `visible` data binding that will hide the table when there are no items left in the `cartItems` array.

When the book index page was created, hiding the table was accomplished via a Razor `if` statement. Knockout is being used here because the user can dynamically delete row elements. After the table, there is an `info` `div` that contains a similar `visible` binding, but will only display when there are no items in the cart.

A `foreach` Knockout binding is created that will loop through the `cartItems` array. A `beforeRemove` callback function is defined that will call the `fadeOut` function from the ViewModel. This callback will do the opposite of the callback that was added in the cart summary to fade in elements when they are added.

Inside the `foreach`, an HTML link is defined that will take the user to the book details page. Previously, when a similar link to this was created, the foreach was being done by Razor providing server-side access to the ID to build the URL. Because this link will be created inside a Knockout `foreach`, the ID needs to be dynamically appended to the end of the `Book/Details` URL. This is a very common behavior when building an index page, so because of this I've created another custom binding called `append` `ToHref` that accepts a property to append to the URL defined.

The next column contains the unit price of the book and is data bound with the `text` binding. The column after this reuses the previously created `upsert-cart-item` custom component, passing in the current `cartItem` being looped using the `$data` property of the `foreach` context. This time, the `showButton` is set to false because I only want the Update button to show when the quantity is changed.

The subTotal is data bound in the next column. This column will dynamically recalculate when the quantity is changed. The final column contains a delete button. It is using the click data binding and will call the deleteCartItem function. It is prefixed with the $parent context because when inside a foreach binding, the current context is the item being looped. Using $parent will go to the first level outside of this where the function resides in the ViewModel.

After the foreach loop ends, the table is closed. Outside of the table is a progress bar that will be displayed when the delete button is clicked, providing feedback to the user that something is happening.

The carts total is bound to a header tag using the text binding. This value will also be dynamically recalculated when either the quantity changes or an item is removed from the cartItems array.

The shared _CartItemForm is included next that contains the previously created template for the custom component. And finally, the JavaScript includes the yet-to-be-created CartDetailViewModel, as well as the CartItemViewModel for the custom component. The model is then serialized, the CartDetailViewModel is created, and the Knockout bindings are applied. The CartDetailViewModel will be created in the next section. Figure 18-1 contains an example of the fully functional cart details page.

Figure 18-1. Cart summary

Knockout for the Cart Details

The previous section introduced a new custom data binding called appendToHref. This has been added to the existing *knockout.custom.js* file and is shown in Example 18-3.

Example 18-3. Updated knockout.custom.js

```
ko.bindingHandlers.appendToHref = {
  init: function (element, valueAccessor) {
    var currentHref = $(element).attr('href');
```

```
      $(element).attr('href', currentHref + '/' + valueAccessor());
    }
  }

ko.bindingHandlers.isDirty = {
  init: function (element, valueAccessor, allBindings, viewModel, bindingContext) {
    var originalValue = ko.unwrap(valueAccessor());

    var interceptor = ko.pureComputed(function () {
      return (bindingContext.$data.showButton !== undefined &&
          bindingContext.$data.showButton)
        || originalValue != valueAccessor()();
    });

    ko.applyBindingsToNode(element, {
      visible: interceptor
    });
  }
};

ko.extenders.subTotal = function (target, multiplier) {
  target.subTotal = ko.observable();

  function calculateTotal(newValue) {
    target.subTotal((newValue * multiplier).toFixed(2));
  };

  calculateTotal(target());

  target.subscribe(calculateTotal);

  return target;
};

ko.observableArray.fn.total = function () {
  return ko.pureComputed(function () {
    var runningTotal = 0;

    for (var i = 0; i < this().length; i++) {
      runningTotal += parseFloat(this()[i].quantity.subTotal());
    }

    return runningTotal.toFixed(2);
  }, this);
};
```

Just like the isDirty custom binding, the appendToHref is added to the ko.binding
Handlers. This time when the init function is defined, it only accepts the first two
parameters: the element and the valueAccessor. Because the other parameters are
not needed in this binding, I have omitted them.

Using jQuery, the current value of the element's `href` attribute is stored in a local variable. This value is used to update the element's `href` by appending the value added in the data binding.

To complete the client-side portion of the cart detail functionality, the `CartDetail` `ViewModel` needs to be created inside the *Scripts/ViewsModels* folder as shown in Example 18-4.

Example 18-4. CartDetailViewModel

```
function CartDetailViewModel(model) {
  var self = this;

  self.sending = ko.observable(false);

  self.cart = model;

  for (var i = 0; i < self.cart.cartItems.length; i++) {
    self.cart.cartItems[i].quantity = ko.observable(self.cart.cartItems[i].quantity)
                    .extend({ subTotal: self.cart.cartItems[i].book.salePrice });
  }

  self.cart.cartItems = ko.observableArray(self.cart.cartItems);

  self.cart.total = self.cart.cartItems.total();

  self.cartItemBeingChanged = null;

  self.deleteCartItem = function (cartItem) {
    self.sending(true);

    self.cartItemBeingChanged = cartItem;

    $.ajax({
      url: '/api/cartitems',
      type: 'delete',
      contentType: 'application/json',
      data: ko.toJSON(cartItem)
    })
    .success(self.successfulDelete)
    .error(self.errorSave)
    .complete(function () { self.sending(false) });
  };

  self.successfulDelete = function (data) {
    $('.body-content').prepend('<div class="alert alert-success">
      <strong>Success!</strong> The item has been deleted from your cart.</div>');

    self.cart.cartItems.remove(self.cartItemBeingChanged);

    cartSummaryViewModel.deleteCartItem(ko.toJS(self.cartItemBeingChanged));
```

```
      self.cartItemBeingChanged = null;
  };

  self.errorSave = function () {
    $('.body-content').prepend('<div class="alert alert-danger">
<strong>Error!</strong> There was an error updating the item to your cart.</div>');
  };

  self.fadeOut = function (element) {
    $(element).fadeOut(1000, function () {
      $(element).remove();
    });
  };
};
```

The start of the ViewModel looks quite similar to the `CartSummaryViewModel`. The `cartItems` are looped through, and the quantity is converted to an observable property and extended to use the previously created `subTotal` extension. The `cartItems` array is then converted into an observable array, and the cart total is stored in a variable leveraging the custom total function for observable arrays.

A nullable `cartItemBeingChanged` variable is defined. This variable is set inside the `deleteCartItem` function and will be used upon successful deletion to remove the element from the `cartItems` array. More on this in a moment.

The `deleteCartItem` is defined next. It works the same as previously defined AJAX requests. It marks the `sending` observable as true to display the progress bar and hide the delete buttons from being clicked multiple times. The AJAX request is then defined next. It goes to the same `api/cartitems` as the add and update requests went before; however, this time the request type is defined as `delete`. On successful save, the function `successfulDelete` will be called. If an error occurs, the `errorSave` function is called. In all scenarios, the complete function is defined to set the `sending` observable back to false, hiding the progress bar.

The `successfulDelete` function adds a success alert on the page, informing the user that the item has been removed from the cart. The previously set `cartItemBeing Changed` variable is used to remove the element from the array. This works because Knockout is able to remove the reference from the array. This way may seem "hacky," but I prefer it to the alternative approach that would require looping through the `car tItems` array, finding a match based on the `cartItem` ID, and then calling the remove function on that item.

This function also calls a `deleteCartItem` function in the global `CartSummaryViewMo del` (shown in Example 18-5).

The errorSave function adds an error alert message to inform the user the item was not removed from the cart.

The final function, fadeOut, is called by Knockout before an element is removed from the cartItems array. This function uses the element and applies the jQuery UI fadeout function over a period of one second. When the jQuery fade completes, the element is removed from the HTML.

Example 18-5 updates the existing CartSummaryViewModel to add the deleteCartItem function.

Example 18-5. Updated CartSummaryViewModel

```
function CartSummaryViewModel(model) {
  var self = this;

  self.cart = model;

  for (var i = 0; i < self.cart.cartItems.length; i++) {
    var cartItem = self.cart.cartItems[i];
    cartItem.quantity = ko.observable(cartItem.quantity)
                    .extend({ subTotal: cartItem.book.salePrice });
  }

  self.cart.cartItems = ko.observableArray(self.cart.cartItems);

  self.cart.total = self.cart.cartItems.total();

  self.updateCartItem = function (cartItem) {
    var isNewItem = true;

    for (var i = 0; i < self.cart.cartItems().length; i++) {
      if (self.cart.cartItems()[i].id == cartItem.id) {
        self.cart.cartItems()[i].quantity(cartItem.quantity);
        isNewItem = false;
        break;
      }
    }

    if (isNewItem) {
      cartItem.quantity = ko.observable(cartItem.quantity)
                  .extend({ subTotal: cartItem.book.salePrice });
      self.cart.cartItems.push(cartItem);
    }
  };

  self.deleteCartItem = function (cartItem) {
    for (var i = 0; i < self.cart.cartItems().length; i++) {
      if (self.cart.cartItems()[i].id == cartItem.id) {
        self.cart.cartItems.remove(self.cart.cartItems()[i]);
```

```
        break;
      }
    }
  };

  self.showCart = function () {
    $('#cart').popover('toggle');
  };

  self.fadeIn = function (element) {
    setTimeout(function () {
      $('#cart').popover('show');

      $(element).slideDown(function () {
        setTimeout(function () {
          $('#cart').popover('hide');
        }, 2000);
      });
    }, 100);
  };

  $('#cart').popover({
    html: true,
    content: function () {
      return $('#cart-summary').html();
    },
    title: 'Cart Details',
    placement: 'bottom',
    animation: true,
    trigger: 'manual'
  });
};

if (cartSummaryData !== undefined) {
  var cartSummaryViewModel = new CartSummaryViewModel(cartSummaryData);
  ko.applyBindings(cartSummaryViewModel, document.getElementById("cart-details"));
} else {
  $('.body-content').prepend('<div class="alert alert-danger">
        <strong>Error!</strong> Could not find cart summary.</div>');
}
```

As you can see, this function uses my alternative suggestion and loops through the cartItems array matching on the item's ID. When a match is found, the item is removed from the observable array, and the loop is exited.

Removing the cart item will cause the cart total to be recalculated.

Completing the Shopping Cart

The shopping cart is almost completed. The final changes are needed in the Web API CartItemsController. Example 18-6 contains an updated CartItemsController.

Example 18-6. Updated CartItemsController

```
using ShoppingCart.Models;
using ShoppingCart.Services;
using ShoppingCart.ViewModels;
using System;
using System.Collections.Generic;
using System.Linq;
using System.Net;
using System.Net.Http;
using System.Web.Http;

namespace ShoppingCart.Controllers.Api
{
  public class CartItemsController : ApiController
  {
    private readonly CartItemService _cartItemService = new CartItemService();

    public CartItemsController()
    {
      AutoMapper.Mapper.CreateMap<Cart, CartViewModel>();
      AutoMapper.Mapper.CreateMap<CartItem, CartItemViewModel>();
      AutoMapper.Mapper.CreateMap<Book, BookViewModel>();

      AutoMapper.Mapper.CreateMap<CartItemViewModel, CartItem>();
      AutoMapper.Mapper.CreateMap<BookViewModel, Book>();
      AutoMapper.Mapper.CreateMap<AuthorViewModel, Author>();
      AutoMapper.Mapper.CreateMap<CategoryViewModel, Category>();
    }

    public CartItemViewModel Post(CartItemViewModel cartItem)
    {
      var newCartItem = _cartItemService.AddToCart(
                  AutoMapper.Mapper.Map<CartItemViewModel, CartItem>(cartItem));

      return AutoMapper.Mapper.Map<CartItem, CartItemViewModel>(newCartItem);
    }

    public CartItemViewModel Put(CartItemViewModel cartItem)
    {
      _cartItemService.UpdateCartItem(
                  AutoMapper.Mapper.Map<CartItemViewModel, CartItem>(cartItem));

      return cartItem;
    }

    public CartItemViewModel Delete(CartItemViewModel cartItem)
    {
      _cartItemService.DeleteCartItem(
                  AutoMapper.Mapper.Map<CartItemViewModel, CartItem>(cartItem));

      return cartItem;
```

```
    }
    protected override void Dispose(bool disposing)
    {
      if (disposing)
      {
        _cartItemService.Dispose();
      }
      base.Dispose(disposing);
    }
  }
}
```

Two new functions were added: Put and Delete. The Put function is called when the update button is clicked and accepts the CartItemViewModel being updated. This function maps the ViewModel to the CartItemModel and calls the UpdateCartItem method in the CartItemService.

The Delete function works the same way with the exception that it calls the Delete CartItem method in the CartService. Both functions return the CartItemViewModel back. It doesn't need to be mapped back because it remains unchanged.

The final changes need to be made to the existing CartItemService as shown in Example 18-7.

Example 18-7. Updated CartItemService

```
using ShoppingCart.DAL;
using ShoppingCart.Models;
using System;
using System.Collections.Generic;
using System.Data.Entity;
using System.Linq;

namespace ShoppingCart.Services
{
  public class CartItemService : IDisposable
  {
    private ShoppingCartContext _db = new ShoppingCartContext();

    public CartItem GetByCartIdAndBookId(int cartId, int bookId)
    {
      return _db.CartItems.SingleOrDefault(ci => ci.CartId == cartId &&
          ci.BookId == bookId);
    }

    public CartItem AddToCart(CartItem cartItem)
    {
      var existingCartItem = GetByCartIdAndBookId(cartItem.CartId, cartItem.BookId);
```

```
    if (null == existingCartItem)
    {
      _db.Entry(cartItem).State = EntityState.Added;
      existingCartItem = cartItem;
    }
    else
    {
      existingCartItem.Quantity += cartItem.Quantity;
    }

    _db.SaveChanges();

    return existingCartItem;
  }

  public void UpdateCartItem(CartItem cartItem)
  {
    _db.Entry(cartItem).State = EntityState.Modified;
    _db.SaveChanges();
  }

  public void DeleteCartItem(CartItem cartItem)
  {
    _db.Entry(cartItem).State = EntityState.Deleted;
    _db.SaveChanges();
  }

  public void Dispose()
  {
    _db.Dispose();
  }
 }
}
```

The two functions, UpdateCartItem and DeleteCartItem, are nearly identical. One marks the item as updated in the ShoppingCartContext while the other marks it as deleted. SaveChanges is then called to commit the changes to the database.

Summary

The shopping cart is now fully functional. Users can browse the catalog of books, and when they find one they like, they can add it to the shopping cart. The cart summary is animated into view, providing the user with feedback on the newly added item.

Clicking the shopping cart item displays the summary of items in their cart with a total and a button to view the full details. Clicking the full details will direct the users to a new page that contains a table of the items in their cart. The item's quantity can be changed or removed completely from the cart. In either case, the totals are automatically recalculated by leveraging Knockout observables.

The shopping cart used a lot of the great features of Knockout—reusable custom components, bindings, functions, and extensions—to build a nice user interface.

This book has attempted to demonstrate a variety of the features of the three technologies used—ASP.NET MVC 5, Bootstrap, and Knockout.js—both together and separately. I've attempted to pass on best practices and my personal experiences having used these three technologies every day for nearly two years.

Mixing three technologies can be a big balancing act. The biggest takeaway I've learned is to constantly analyze what you are trying to accomplish and pick the right mix of the technologies being used. This is important, because it can be easy to use Knockout for every page in the website. But as I've demonstrated, I use it sparingly where dynamic interaction is required. Picking the right technology for the job will provide a much better user experience than blindly picking one and sticking with it.

When it comes to using client-side libraries like Knockout, there is a lot of rave over single-page web applications. I think they look and act quite nice; however, I don't think it is the be-all and end-all of web design either. In certain situations, they make sense, and in others, they don't. If the website contains a single focus, single-page designs are great; why direct the user away when the UI can be updated dynamically? When the context of the pages change, though, I think it makes more sense to avoid the single-page design. Using the shopping cart as an example, the book details page and the cart details page contain similar functionality; however, what the user is attempting to accomplish is quite different. Just like picking the right technology, picking the right design is equally important.

I hope you have enjoyed this book as much as I enjoyed writing it. You can find me online through my blog End Your If (*http://www.endyourif.com*) and on Twitter (*https://twitter.com/endyourif*), where I would be happy to answer questions about the book.

Index

About the Author

Jamie Munro is the author of *Knockout.js: Building Dynamic Client-Side Web Applications, 20 Recipes for Programming MVC 3,* and *20 Recipes for Programming PhoneGap.* He has been developing websites and web applications for over 15 years. For the past eight years, Jamie has been acting as a lead developer by mentoring younger developers to enhance their skills.

Using his love of mentoring people, Jamie began his writing career on his personal blog back in 2009. As the success of Jamie's blog grew, he turned his writing passion to books about web development in hopes that his many years of experience could be passed on to his readers.

Colophon

The animal on the cover of *ASP.NET MVC 5 with Bootstrap and Knockout.js* is a checkerboard wrasse (*Halichoeres hortulanus*). This common fish can be found anywhere from the Red Sea to the Great Barrier Reef, and also goes by marbled or Hortulanus wrasse.

Both sexes of this species sport the distinctive checkerboard pattern from which it gets its name, but only the males have a bright yellow dorsal stripe as well. Juveniles are black and white, but they gradually change color and develop the pattern as they grow.

The checkerboard wrasse prefers to live in lagoons and near seaward reefs at depths from one to 30 meters. They mostly eat mollusks, crustaceans, and sea urchins, and males tend to be very territorial about their habitats.

Due to its bright pattern, medium size (anywhere between one and five inches), varied diet, and easy availability, the checkerboard wrasse is popular in home aquariums.

Many of the animals on O'Reilly covers are endangered; all of them are important to the world. To learn more about how you can help, go to *animals.oreilly.com.*

The cover image is from Wood's *Natural History.* The cover fonts are URW Typewriter and Guardian Sans. The text font is Adobe Minion Pro; the heading font is Adobe Myriad Condensed; and the code font is Dalton Maag's Ubuntu Mono.

Get even more for your money.

Join the O'Reilly Community, and register the O'Reilly books you own. It's free, and you'll get:

- $4.99 ebook upgrade offer
- 40% upgrade offer on O'Reilly print books
- Membership discounts on books and events
- Free lifetime updates to ebooks and videos
- Multiple ebook formats, DRM FREE
- Participation in the O'Reilly community
- Newsletters
- Account management
- 100% Satisfaction Guarantee

Signing up is easy:

1. Go to: oreilly.com/go/register
2. Create an O'Reilly login.
3. Provide your address.
4. Register your books.

Note: English-language books only

To order books online:
oreilly.com/store

For questions about products or an order:
orders@oreilly.com

To sign up to get topic-specific email announcements and/or news about upcoming books, conferences, special offers, and new technologies:
elists@oreilly.com

For technical questions about book content:
booktech@oreilly.com

To submit new book proposals to our editors:
proposals@oreilly.com

O'Reilly books are available in multiple DRM-free ebook formats. For more information:
oreilly.com/ebooks

Have it your way.